BITES ON A BOARD

Anne Daelle

photographs by **Alexandra DeFurio**

GIBBS SMITH
TO ENRICH AND INSPIRE HUMANKIND

First Edition
23 22 21   10 9

Text © 2017 Anni Daulter
Photographs © 2017 Alexandra DeFurio

Published by
Gibbs Smith
P.O. Box 667
Layton, Utah 84041

1.800.835.4993 orders
www.gibbs-smith.com

Designed by Sheryl Dickert
Food Styling by Anni Daulter, Delicious Gratitude
Printed and bound in China
Gibbs Smith books are printed on either recycled, 100%
post-consumer waste, FSC-certified papers or on
paper produced from sustainable PEFC-certified forest/
controlled wood source. Learn more at www.pefc.org.

Library of Congress Cataloging-in-Publication Data

Names: Daulter, Anni, author. | DeFurio, Alexandra,
photographer.
Title: Bites on a board / Anni Daulter ; photographs by
Alexandra DeFurio.
Description: First edition. | Layton, Utah : Gibbs Smith,
[2017]
Identifiers: LCCN 2016031439 | ISBN 9781423645740
Subjects: LCSH: Appetizers. | Food presentation. | LCGFT:
Cookbooks.
Classification: LCC TX740 .D3349 2017 | DDC 641.8½—dc23
LC record available at https://lccn.loc.gov/2016031439

This sweet book is for all the foodies out there who want to jump into a new culinary trend and make some amazing food in the process. Also to my husband Tim and my children; Lotus, Zoe, Bodhi; and River—you are all my heart and soul!

BITES ON A
BOARD

bites on a board

is an exciting dining trend that has culinary masters expanding their menus to explore possibilities, and home cooks excited to dive in and play with creative serving options. This book has unique recipes that are inspired from many lands, satisfy homespun cravings, awaken the sweet tooth, and even flirt with healing properties. Service on funky boards gives the dining experience a unique twist, and invites you to dive into the beauty world of food styling while feeding your guests amazing foods!

So pull out your board bravado and start a community dinner trend with your local foodie tribe. Push your creativity to new limits and have fun with your own styling of these delicious recipes.

BOARDS

Your boards are where the fun starts, but certainly *not* where it ends. As you flip through *Bites on a Board*, you will find many juicy board ideas, and all of them work to create a particular feel and ambiance for the food itself. While we call all of the presentations, *boards*, you do not literally have to use a wooden board to display this conceptual dining trend. Invite your creativity to the party to see what you can come up with—platters, planks, trays, and even bowls will work.

Whether you choose a traditional wooden plank for a charcuterie display, or twist-up the presentation with a colorful ceramic for a lush board, or get cultured with a silver-plated party for an Indian-spiced board, you are sure to make a dining splash with all of your culinary friends.

If you use wooden boards or planks, make sure to simply wash them with a wet cloth and a light natural soap. Do not let them soak in water or put them in the dishwasher, as the wood will ripple and will eventually be ruined.

STYLING

You have likely heard the saying, "We eat with our eyes first." This popular prose speaks to our desire to have our food look delectable before we put it into our mouth. We worked hard to make these boards look like something you want to make, and that is all done with fun props, great food, and a little sprinkle of fairy dust.

You may not have an actual food-styling background, but you can use this book to push your presentations to new levels. Entice your guests with dainty lush boards using a color-inspired palette, bountiful rustic wood boards full of comfort foods, or boards based on an international theme with exotic flavors and textures. There are various styling tips throughout the book that will help inspire and guide you to a creative platform that will have you playing with food before every meal!

STYLING BASICS

COLOR MATTERS Color can be as exciting as the food itself, and can be the foundation for your styling that gives the food an extra shot of vibrancy. Monochromatic tones have a dramatic effect. For example, if all the foods for your board are inspired by reds, the presentation should attempt to match that intention. Placing foods of various colors next to ones that are complimentary is also a food-styling basic that can take you a long way in your overall presentation.

THRIFT IT Shopping at thrift stores to find props for your boards and styling is a great way to go because you can find styling goodies that are usually inexpensive and quirky. You will be able to score anything from handmade ceramics to antique silver spoons to old jars and containers that cannot be found anywhere else. So take a moment to find out where your local thrift stores are located, and have a fun treasure hunting day.

OLD IS THE NEW HIP Mixing antique items with modern designs gives styling a fresh perspective. For example, use enamel pieces paired with trendy feathers and crystals to give the presentation a funky spiritual vibe that is both beautiful and cutting edge. Containers found at antique shops used to hold delicate food provides a fun juxtaposition to your display.

VESSELS AND TEXTURES Everything and anything can be vessels for the foods on your board layouts, and getting creative with this is the key. For example, take the label off an old soup can and give a fun feel to a handful of sweet potato fries. Use Mason jars with tape labels and old antique bowls for sauces and jams to give your styling a rustic feel. Grab an old book or a newspaper and use the pages as texture under your food display, or grab an old linen cloth to give your presentation a romantic feel. Don't be afraid to push your limits. Experiment with upcycling and use mix-matched vessels to create an artistic container for the board recipes.

PROPORTION When styling a food presentation, proportion matters. You don't want to have two things shaped alike placed on the board, or items that are very large next to items that are very small. You will also want to keep in mind proportion of the vessels you choose to hold your food and where they are placed on your boards.

TRENDSETTER
BOARDS

trendsetter

a person or thing that establishes
a new trend or fashion

BOARD IT UP: Trendsetter boards will be funky, stylish, and current. Think cutting edge and quirky, with a twist of your own personal flare. When plating these boards, flirt with high end, but keep it simple, clean, and artistic. The beauty of these boards will be in your creative presentation, but remember that taste always comes first. The trendsetter boards should say a little something about your personal style.

Grilled Pineapple

Huli Huli
Salmon Skewers

Poke Avocado Salad with Edible Flowers

ISLAND DAYS

THE INSPIRATION The mundaneness of life can invite a stirring within you that seeks island days with dreamy moments of warm sun, soft breezes, crystal blue waters, and delectable bites to bring about a needed recharge. The trendsetter wants beauty to drip from every plate, while keeping the food fresh, flirty, and fun. Take a trip to the islands with this board of clean foods that are beautiful and tasty. Relax into creating this board and allow yourself to be inspired by your tropical day dreams.

STYLING TIPS You can serve grilled pineapple as shown on the board, or create skewers from the recipe on page 13. Whichever you choose, grill the pineapple last so it is nicely warm to compliment the cold poke salad and salty huli huli salmon. Because you could have 2 skewered items on this board, keep proportion in mind. Maybe use a tin can to hold up the huli huli salmon while the pineapple is placed on the board.

Poke Avocado Salad with Edible Flowers

SERVES 2

½ pound sushi grade ahi (tuna)

1 ½ teaspoons sesame oil

1 teaspoon soy sauce

1 tablespoon ponzu sauce

¼ teaspoon each salt and pepper

½ teaspoon black sesame seeds

2 green onions, thinly sliced

1 avocado, cubed

½ lemon, juiced

A handful of edible flowers

Rinse and completely dry the ahi with a paper towel. Cut into ¼-inch cubes and place into a glass mixing bowl.

Add the sesame oil, soy sauce, ponzu sauce, salt, and pepper and gently mix. Add sesame seeds, green onions, and avocado and lightly combine.

Transfer the salad into the serving bowl for your board and top with lemon juice and edible flowers arranged in a beautiful style. You can also place the salad into an individual bowl for each guest. Refrigerate until ready to board up.

There are many types of edible wild flowers, including marigolds, nasturtiums, all-season violas, lilacs, elder flowers, and dandelions. It is really up to you to determine what presentation you want to make with your flowers.

Huli Huli Salmon Skewers

SERVES 4

½ cup packed brown sugar

¼ cup ketchup

¼ cup reduced-sodium soy sauce

⅓ cup chicken broth

Pinch of each salt and pepper

1 teaspoon minced fresh ginger

1 teaspoon minced garlic

2 pounds salmon fillets cut into 2-inch chunks

Skewer sticks

2 green onions, thinly sliced

In a small mixing bowl, combine brown sugar, ketchup, soy sauce, broth, salt and pepper, ginger, and garlic. Reserve 1 cup of the sauce for basting the salmon while grilling.

Place the sauce and salmon into a large ziplock bag, and marinate for at least 3–4 hours.

When ready to grill, thread the salmon chunks onto the skewers. Grill, covered, on medium heat for approximately 6–8 minutes on each side until no longer pink. Occasionally baste the salmon while grilling, and once done, sprinkle the fish with green onions.

Huli means "turn" in Hawaiian, and therefore the idea is to keep turning the salmon to let the flavors evenly cook.

Grilled Pineapple

SERVES 2

½ whole fresh pineapple,
    cubed

½ yellow onion, cubed

Skewer sticks

Thread the pineapple and onion cubes onto skewers, alternating between the pineapple and onion.

Grill on low heat to get nice grill marks on the skewered food, turning every couple of minutes until the onions are well cooked. These also look great taken off the skewers and stacked on the board.

Pop these onto the grill just as the salmon is almost done.

d Asparagus Spears
with Amino Garlic Sauce

Peppered
Aged Cheddar
Cheese

Kale Cumin Chips

Pan-Fried Wild Mushrooms with Walnuts and Rustic Toast

THE WILD UNKNOWN

THE INSPIRATION You have a wild beating heart that answers the call of the deep, dark woods. Somewhere, a wolf howls and a hawk cries and something magic in you stirs. This is a board with the earthy taste of woodlands and fields; an ode to the wild untamed edges in your life. Awaken these secret yearnings with spice and the loamy scent of mushrooms.

STYLING TIPS Serve this collection on a piece of wild wood with a moody red wine. Add elements of moss, smoky quartz crystals, or even feathers to enhance the ambiance of this woodsy meal.

Cumin Kale Chips

SERVES 4

2 bunches Lacinato kale

1 tablespoon sesame seeds

1 tablespoon cumin seeds

¼ teaspoon celery seeds

1 teaspoon ground cumin

1 teaspoon smoked paprika

1 teaspoon coconut oil

Flaked sea salt, to taste

Cracked black pepper, to taste

Preheat oven to 300 degrees F. Wash and completely dry the kale.

Tear the kale into bite-size pieces. You may want to remove the tough, stringy center. It is perfectly edible, but some prefer a less chewy crunch to the chips. Place the kale into a large mixing bowl and set aside.

In a dry skillet over medium heat, toast all of the seeds and ground spices. Keep the pan moving in a gentle swirling motion so the spices do not burn. When seeds and spices are fragrant and warmed, remove from the heat and set aside.

Melt the coconut oil and gently massage into the nooks and crevices of the kale.

Toss the spices into the bowl with the kale and make sure everything is evenly dispersed and well coated. Place the kale in a single layer on 2 baking sheets. Bake for about 25 minutes, swapping the trays halfway through baking.

Roasted Asparagus Spears with Amino Garlic Sauce

SERVES 4

2 bunches asparagus

2 tablespoons olive oil

Flaked sea salt, to taste

Cracked black pepper, to taste

½ lemon

Amino Garlic Sauce

¼ cup coconut vinegar

¼ cup coconut aminos

¼ cup water

¼ cup toasted sesame oil

1 teaspoon honey

1 clove garlic, crushed

1 spring onion, finely chopped

Preheat oven to 425 degrees F.

Wash the asparagus and snap off the woody ends. Rub the olive oil onto the spears so that they are well coated.

Spread the asparagus into 1 layer on a baking sheet. Sprinkle with the salt and pepper. Squeeze lemon over the top.

Roast in oven for 15–20 minutes.

Amino Garlic Sauce

While the asparagus spears are roasting, blend together all the ingredients except the onion. Pour into a small serving container and garnish with the onion. To serve, drizzle over roasted asparagus.

Pan-Fried Wild Mushrooms with Walnuts and Rustic Toast

SERVES 4

2 cups wild mushrooms

1 cup walnuts

2 tablespoons butter

1 clove garlic

3 tablespoons chopped
flat-leaf parsley

Cracked black pepper, to
taste

Flaked sea salt, to taste

Fresh Parmesan cheese,
grated

1 loaf sourdough,
pumpernickel, or whole-
grain bread, sliced and
toasted

Prepare the mushrooms by giving them a light brush, removing any dirt. Roughly chop them. Roughly chop the walnuts.

Heat the butter in a frying pan over medium heat. Once the butter is bubbling, add the mushrooms and nuts. Cook gently until golden, and then add the garlic. Let infuse and meld together for another 2 minutes. Add parsley and turn to coat. Do not burn the garlic.

Finish the dish by seasoning with pepper, salt, and a sprinkling of Parmesan. Serve on the warm toasted bread.

FINISHING THE BOARD

Add a generous wedge of peppered aged cheddar to your board to balance out the meal.

Random Nuts

Avocado

Red Quinoa

Over Easy Egg

Beet Chips

Heirloom Tomato

ALL THE YES, IN A BOWL

THE INSPIRATION Incredibly virtuous real foods gather together to nourish your body and soul. These sharing bowls are packed with goodness in every way. Why not celebrate with an affirmation gratitude practice as you honor friends and family with these treasures. Serve them with a modern retro twist using mismatched bowls in the same color scheme and use an old baking dish as your board. Hand write a special affirmation to accompany each bowl.

STYLING TIPS Feature the board with all the foods placed together in the serving bowl as well as small portions of some of the foods separated out and artistically placed on the board. Make as many bowls as needed to serve your guests.

Beet Chips

SERVES 4

1 golden beet

1 Chioggia beet

1 red beet

1 teaspoon olive oil

Sea salt and black pepper,
  to taste

Preheat oven to 375 degrees F.

Wash and peel the beets. Slice as thinly as possible. A mandolin makes this very easy—otherwise a sharp knife and patient practice are your best tools.

Massage the olive oil into the beets so they are well covered and glistening. Spread the beets in a single layer on 2 baking sheets and sprinkle with salt and pepper.

Bake for about 15–20 minutes, switching pans halfway through. Keep a close eye on the beets because they can burn very quickly towards the end of the cooking time.

Toasted Nuts

MAKES ½ CUP NUTS

½ cup raw mixed nuts (pine nuts, hazelnuts, pecans, cashews, and walnuts)

1 tablespoon butter

Place a skillet on medium heat and melt butter. Once melted, add the nuts to the pan. Toss to coat in butter. Keep the nuts moving so they don't burn, and cook until golden and toasted.

Balanced Bowl

SERVES 4 SHARING

1 cup red quinoa

2 cups water or stock

Toasted Nuts page 22

1 tablespoon olive oil

Squeeze of lemon

1 ripe avocado

1 heirloom tomato or 1 cup
   heirloom cherry tomatoes

Juice of 1 lime

1 tablespoon butter

1 egg

Salt and pepper, to taste

Dash of your favorite hot
   sauce

Rinse the quinoa in cold water. Add to pan over medium heat and dry toast the quinoa until it starts to warm and crackle. Keep stirring so it doesn't burn.

Add the water or stock and bring to a boil. Once boiling, turn down heat to a simmer and cover. Test after 20 minutes to see if it is fluffy and to your liking. If you need to, drain off any excess water. Stir in Toasted Nuts.

Dress quinoa with olive oil and a squeeze of lemon. Layer in bottom of your serving dish.

FINISHING THE BOARD

Peel and cube the avocado and add to bowl. Dice heirloom tomato and add to bowl. Squeeze lime juice over the top.

To cook egg, heat 1 tablespoon butter in pan over medium heat. Once melted, crack egg into pan. Once the white is firm and cooked, flip the egg to lightly cook on the other side. Over easy has a runny yolk, so don't cook longer than a minute once you've flipped it. Add to top of serving bowl. Layer the beet chips on top.

Season everything with salt and pepper. Finish with a dash of hot sauce if you like.

pickled

preserved or steeped in brine or other liquid

BOARD IT UP: Pickled boards will be home-spun with a farm-to-table quality about them. Think fresh and plentiful when plating these planks. When you are styling your pickled boards, you will need tin cans, newspapers, parchment paper, various-size Mason jars, and whatever old/new vintage-looking containers you can muster.

Half Sour Pickles

Fermented Gingery Lemonade

Preserved
Salted Lemons

Spinach and Feta Pie

FERMENTED FARMERS MARKET

INSPIRATION The delightful mosaic of sights and smells of the seasonal farmers market brings a feeling of romance and whimsy to your life. This board captures the beauty of fleeting local discoveries and entices all your senses into the adventure. Pickling, fermenting, and preserving helps keep the foods vibrant, and naturally accents their flavors in exciting ways. This board is fun to accent with Mason jars and natural linens.

STYLING TIPS Use the farmers market for your inspiration for creating this board. Loose wild flowers or fresh lemon slices floating about on the board, a Mason jar full of pickles, and rustic containers with salted lemons will keep your presentation inspired by farm fresh goodness and ready for back porch chitchats. You can also add a bowl of Citrus-Pickled Artichokes (page 28) for more flavor.

Citrus-Pickled Artichokes

SERVES 4

4 small artichokes

4 cloves garlic

5 whole black peppercorns

3 cups white wine vinegar

½ cup lemon juice

¼ cup honey

1 teaspoon chili flakes

1 bunch oregano

1 small orange, quartered

Olive oil

Prepare the artichokes by trimming the ends off the leaves and cutting in half. Remove the choke and cut in half again so the artichokes are quartered.

Simmer the garlic, peppercorns, vinegar, and lemon juice in a saucepan. Boil for about 2 minutes. Take off heat and mix in honey.

Place the artichoke pieces, chili flakes, oregano, and orange in a clean Mason jar and top with the marinade. Marinate for 48 hours and then top with a thin layer of olive oil .

Half-Sour Pickles

MAKES 1 POUND PICKLES

1 pound small pickling
    cucumbers, quartered

2 cups water

1 heaped tablespoon kosher
    salt

5 cloves garlic

1 head dill

8 black peppercorns

1 teaspoon mustard seeds

Sterilize a Mason jar either by running through the dishwasher without soap or by boiling and letting dry. Pack the cucumbers tightly into jar.

In a saucepan, warm the rest of the ingredients together until the salt has dissolved. Pour brine into jar, making sure pickles are well covered, and close the jar

Fermenting is about discovering the taste you like best. Start checking the pickles after 3 days. They usually take 5–9 days. They will begin to soften as they pickle so look for the right balance of sour and crunch for your palate.

Preserved Salted Lemons

MAKES ½ GALLON

8 lemons

8 tablespoons coarse sea
   salt, divided

5 sprigs thyme

3 allspice berries

1 large whole red chile
   pepper

1 cup lemon juice

Olive oil

Sterilize your jar either by running through the dishwasher without soap or by boiling and letting dry. Prepare lemons by washing them and cutting deep crosses into the tops.

Pack each lemon with 1 tablespoon of the salt. Then place into jar. It is okay to firmly push and pack the lemons into the jar. They will be very tight and cozy. Close the jar and allow to rest on the counter for 7–10 days.

Once a good amount of juice has collected, after 7–10 days, press down on the lemons, squeezing the juice to the bottom of the jar. Add all the remaining ingredients except the olive oil. Close the jar and give a shake to combine everything.

Open the jar, press everything down again, and top with a layer of olive oil. Leave for 4–6 weeks or longer.

To use, you can purée everything and add a teaspoon at a time to dishes, or you can take a slice or two as needed.

Preserved lemons are a Mediterranean classic that add a salty vibrancy to many dishes. They also make a wonderful gift if you happen to have an abundance of the golden fruit.

Spinach and Feta Pie

SERVES 4 TO 6

1 red onion, thinly sliced

3 cloves garlic, peeled and
crushed

3 cups fresh spinach

1 vine-ripened tomato,
chopped

2 cups crumbled feta cheese

1 teaspoon nutmeg

1 teaspoon preserved lemon

2 eggs, beaten

Salt and pepper, to taste

1 package phyllo pastry

Olive oil

Paprika

Preheat oven to 350 degrees F.

Slowly caramelize the onion by placing in a saucepan over medium-low heat and cooking for 20–30 minutes, stirring occasionally to prevent sticking.

Add the garlic and cook for another 5 minutes. Add the spinach, tomato, feta cheese, nutmeg, and preserved lemon.

Once spinach begins to wilt, take off heat. Add eggs and season with salt and pepper.

Layer the pastry into the bottom and up the sides of an 8-inch cast iron skillet. Or you can use an 8-inch springform pan. Brush each layer of phyllo with olive oil. Make 3–5 layers in total.

Spoon in all of the filling and gather the phyllo together on the top, scrunching and draping as needed. Brush the swirls and crags with olive oil and sprinkle with paprika. Bake for about 30 minutes until golden and crisp on the outside. Let cool for 10 minutes before serving.

This pie is a wonderful accompaniment to the pickles and tastes fantastic with a teaspoon or two of the preserved lemons and garnished with the artichokes.

Fermented Gingery Lemonade

MAKES ABOUT 2 QUARTS

1 cup honey

5 cups water

1 cup lemon juice

¼ cup fresh ginger juice or ½ cup sliced ginger

½ cup fresh whey

Place all ingredients, except whey, into a large saucepan and simmer for 20–30 minutes. Cool to room temperature and strain. Place liquid in a clean, sterile jar and add whey.

Cover tightly, leave the jar on the counter, and let the magic of fermentation happen for about 3 days then check it. Once it starts to get a little fizzy you know you are close. Keep checking until it has the balance of sweetness, tartness, and fizziness that you like.

Pour into smaller soda bottles that have either a flip-top or screw-top lid.

Keep the soda bottles at room temperature and check every day. This is the tricky part! The carbonation increases very quickly. You need to open the soda bottles every day or they run the risk of exploding. Once they reach a level of carbonation you like, put them in the refrigerator to slow everything down. Once chilled they are ready for drinking.

This is a spicy lemonade to tickle the senses and impress your guests. Feel free to increase the honey for a sweeter, mellower beverage.

Pickled Red Onion with
Miso Skirt Steak Strips

Pickled Ginger and
Sesame Slaw

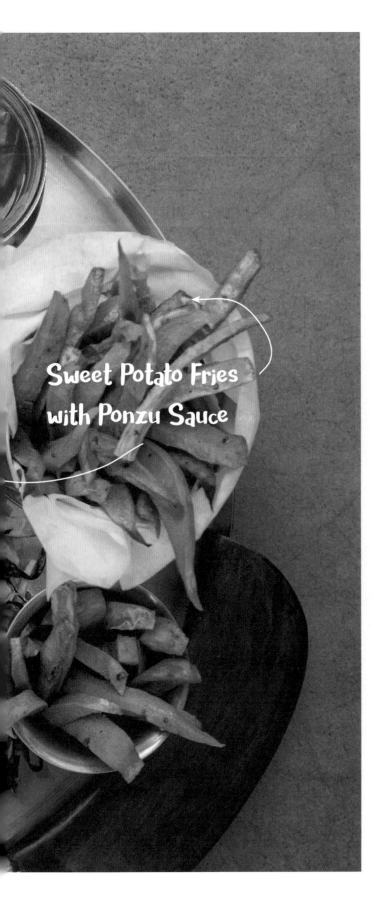

Sweet Potato Fries
with Ponzu Sauce

PICKLE ME FANCY

INSPIRATION Time to kick up your pickles to the refined notch of an elegant evening soirée. This is no rough and tumble market place. Oh no. Pull out a swanky dress and your prettiest platters for this board. Tea lights flirt behind colored glass, the sizzle of the grill and scintillating conversation imbue the food with zest.

STYLING TIPS Compliment the bright colors of the food with sophisticated vintage silver and jewel-like colored glass. Serve with Fermented Strawberry Soda found on page 41.

Pickled Red Onion with Miso Skirt Steak Strips

SERVES 4

Pickled Red Onion

1 teaspoon sugar

½ teaspoon salt

1 cup apple cider vinegar

1 small clove garlic, halved

5 black peppercorns

5 allspice berries

1 star anise

1 medium red onion, thinly sliced

Place all the ingredients, except the onion, into a small saucepan and warm until the sugar dissolves.

Place onion slices and the pickling liquid into a sealable jar or container, and then shake well to mix. Leave in cool place for a minimum of 45 minutes. Keeps well in refrigerator for weeks.

Miso Skirt Steak Strips

SERVES 4

¼ cup organic red miso

1 teaspoon coconut aminos

1 teaspoon hot sweet mustard

1 teaspoon grated peeled ginger

1 teaspoon kosher salt

1 clove garlic, grated

2 tablespoons sesame oil

1 pound grass-fed beef skirt steak

Sea salt and cracked black pepper, to taste

Mix together the miso, coconut aminos, mustard, ginger, salt, garlic, and sesame oil to create a paste. Rub paste into steak and cover in plastic wrap. Let marinate for at least 30 minutes, and no longer than overnight.

When ready to cook, brush grill with a little more oil and let the meat come to room temperature while the grill is heating. Remove steak from marinade and place on grill.

Grill for about 13 minutes on each side—make sure to check it as grill temperatures vary. Once cooked to your liking, remove from grill and let rest for 10 minutes. Slice into strips, season with salt and pepper, and serve with the pickled onion.

The umami flavor of the miso is a bright contrast to the sourness of the onion. It is a versatile marinade that works equally well with vegetables or fish.

Sweet Potato Fries with Ponzu Sauce

SERVES 4

2 large sweet potatoes

1 tablespoon coconut oil

Salt and pepper, to taste

Ponzu Sauce

MAKES ⅓ CUP

⅓ cup soy sauce

1 tablespoon white wine vinegar

2 cloves of garlic, peeled

Preheat oven to 350 degrees F.

Peel and cut sweet potatoes into equal-size fries. Place on a baking sheet, coat with coconut oil, and sprinkle with salt and pepper.

Bake for about 45 minutes, turning occasionally, until crispy.

Ponzu Sauce

Mix all the ingredients together in a bowl. Let infuse for 15 minutes before serving. This sauce gets better after 24 hours, so make ahead if possible.

Pickled Ginger and Sesame Slaw

Pickled Ginger

MAKES ABOUT 1 CUP

1 cup rice vinegar

½ cup sugar

½ cup water

1 teaspoon salt

1 allspice berry

1 star anise

1 cup peeled and thinly sliced ginger*

Sesame Slaw

SERVES 4

1 cup shredded red cabbage

1 cup shredded white cabbage

1 cup grated carrot

¼ cup chopped spring onion

¼ cup Pickled Ginger

¼ cup sesame seeds

¼ cup toasted sesame oil

¼ cup rice vinegar

3 tablespoons honey

Salt and pepper, to taste

Pickled Ginger

In a small saucepan, heat everything together except for the ginger.

Pack ginger into a Mason jar and pour warm liquid over the top. Seal and leave to pickle for at least 2 hours. This gets sweeter the longer it sets, and it keeps very well in the refrigerator.

*A mandolin works great for thinly slicing the ginger

Sesame Slaw

Mix all the vegetables, pickled ginger, and sesame seeds together in a large bowl.

In a separate bowl, whisk together the oil, vinegar, honey, and salt and pepper. Add to the vegetables and thoroughly combine.

Fermented Strawberry Soda

MAKES 2 QUARTS

4 cups organic strawberries, hulled and halved

¼ cup lemon juice

1 cup organic cane sugar

2 quarts pure water

½ cup whey

Place all ingredients, except whey, into a large saucepan and simmer for 20–30 minutes. Cool to room temperature and strain. Place liquid in a clean, sterile jar and add whey.

Cover tightly, leave the jar on the counter, and let the magic of fermentation happen for about 3 days then check it. Once it starts to get a little fizzy you know you are close. Keep checking until it has the balance of sweetness, tartness, and fizziness that you like.

Pour into smaller soda bottles that have either a flip-top or screw-top lid.

Keep the soda bottles at room temperature and check every day. This is the tricky part! The carbonation increases very quickly. You need to open the soda bottles every day or they run the risk of exploding. Once they reach a level of carbonation you like, put them in the refrigerator to slow everything down. Once chilled they are ready for drinking.

Lacto-fermentation uses whey to start the blissfully bubbling process. You can explore other methods such as ginger bugs or kombucha.

Dilly Pickle Fries
with Garlic Aioli

Mini Kobe Beef Sliders

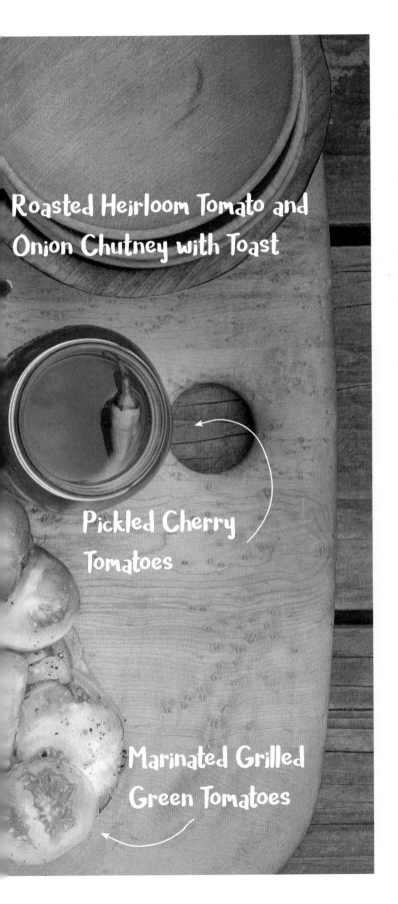

Roasted Heirloom Tomato and Onion Chutney with Toast

Pickled Cherry Tomatoes

Marinated Grilled Green Tomatoes

CURED TOMATO PLANK

INSPIRATION The ripe juicy lushness of sun-ripened tomatoes is one of the highlights of summer. This board is an alluring and light-kissed homage to the halcyon days of golden summer and these jewel-like enticing fruits.

STYLING TIPS To make the tomatoes center stage, keep the color palette neutral with natural fibers and materials. Rather than a whole jar on the board, you can plate the pickles and chutney in smaller dishes.

Pickled Cherry Tomatoes

MAKES 2 PINTS

6 cups assorted cherry tomatoes (yellow, red, green)

1 tablespoon cumin seeds

1 tablespoon mustard seeds

1 tablespoon celery seeds

1 teaspoon caraway seeds

6 black peppercorns

6 cloves garlic, peeled

2 bay leaves

2 small whole dried Thai chile peppers

3 cups apple cider vinegar

1 ½ cups water

2 tablespoons salt

¼ cup sugar

Remove any stems and leaves from tomatoes and wash them. Carefully prick each one a couple times with a thin skewer. This allows the pickle juice to really get into them.

Sterilize 2 pint-size Mason jars either by running through the dishwasher without soap or by boiling and letting dry.

In a dry pan, toast the seeds and peppercorns until fragrant. Keep the pan moving so you do not burn them. Share the toasted spices between the 2 jars and add in the garlic, bay leaves, and chiles.

In a medium saucepan, heat together the vinegar, water, salt, and sugar until the sugar dissolves. While the vinegar is simmering, pack the tomatoes into the jars.

Pour the warm liquid over the tomatoes and seal the jars. The tomatoes are ready to eat after 24 hours, and keep well for weeks in the refrigerator.

These tomatoes are bursting with tang and juice. They make excellent additions to salads and charcuterie boards. The jars make fun gifts.

Roasted Heirloom Tomato and Onion Chutney with Toast

1 pound heirloom tomatoes, hulled and quartered

1 large red onion, sliced

5 cloves garlic, peeled and sliced

2 tablespoons olive oil

½ cup grated carrot

3 tablespoons lemon juice

¼ cup packed brown sugar

¼ cup balsamic vinegar

Salt and pepper, to taste

1 loaf sourdough bread, sliced and toasted

Place all the ingredients, except the bread, into a saucepan over medium-low heat. Gently simmer for 60 minutes, stirring occasionally to prevent sticking. The chutney should be dark, sticky, and thick. Check for seasoning and adjust as needed.

To serve, spread abundantly over sourdough toast and enjoy.

Time and patience give this chutney its bold and rich flavor. Don't rush the alchemy which transforms this into a sublime condiment.

Grilled Marinated Green Tomatoes

SERVES 4 TO 6

¼ cup olive oil

¼ cup white balsamic
vinegar

2 cloves garlic, crushed

1 tablespoon honey

¼ teaspoon salt

1 tablespoon chopped basil

1 tablespoon lemon juice

1 pound green tomatoes, cut
into ¼-inch-thick slices

Sea salt and freshly ground
pepper, to taste

Whisk olive oil, vinegar, garlic, honey, salt, basil, and lemon juice together. Place tomatoes in a large bowl, pour in the marinade, and cover. Give a little shake to coat well and refrigerate for 1 hour.

Grill tomatoes, on medium heat, for 2–3 minutes per side. Arrange on platter and drizzle with a touch of olive oil and season with salt and pepper.

Mini Kobe Beef Sliders

MAKES 12 SLIDERS

1 pound Kobe beef, ground

1 teaspoon garlic powder

1 teaspoon onion powder

1 teaspoon smoked chipotle powder

1 tablespoon coconut aminos

Sea salt and cracked black pepper, to taste

Butter

12 brioche buns

12 dollops Roasted Heirloom Tomato and Onion Chutney page 45

Mix the beef, garlic powder, onion powder, chipotle powder, aminos, and salt and pepper together. Form 12 small patties.

Grill patties on an oiled grill for a couple minutes on each side. Since they are small they will cook fairly quickly. After you have flipped the burgers the first time, place buttered buns on the grill to lightly toast.

Place the burgers on the bottom halves of the buns, add dollop of chutney to each, and top with other half of buns.

Kobe beef has a low fat melting point and a rich flavor. If you can't find it, grass-fed beef or buffalo are good substitutions.

Dilly Pickle Fries with Garlic Aioli

SERVES 4 TO 6

4 cups sunflower oil

1 (32-ounce) jar whole dill
    pickles

2 ½ cups panko
    breadcrumbs

1 teaspoon garlic powder

½ teaspoon chipotle
    powder

¼ teaspoon allspice

½ teaspoon salt

½ teaspoon cracked black
    pepper

1 cup flour

1 ½ cups buttermilk

Garlic Aioli

MAKES 1 CUP

1 cup mayonnaise

Juice of 2 lemons

2 cloves garlic, crushed

Salt and pepper, to taste

In a large deep pot, preheat the oil to 375 degrees F. Using a mandolin or sharp knife, slice the pickles into ¼-inch-thick rounds.

In a large mixing bowl, mix the panko, spices, and salt and pepper. Place the flour in another bowl, and pour the buttermilk into a third bowl.

Begin by dipping each pickle slice into the flour, shaking off any extra. Then dip the floured pickle into the buttermilk, again shaking off any extra. Finally coat in the panko. Once all of the pickles are dressed, begin frying in batches.

To fry, carefully place a few battered pickles into the hot oil. Fry for 2 minutes on the first side then carefully turn and cook for another 2 minutes until golden brown and crispy. When the pickles are ready, scoop them out of the oil with a slotted spoon and drain on paper towels.

Continue to fry in batches until complete. Give the finished pickles a sprinkle of salt and pepper and serve warm with the Garlic Aioli.

Garlic Aioli

Whisk all the ingredients together in a small bowl. Check seasoning and add salt and pepper as needed.

Grilled Summer Squash
and Spring Onions

Pickled Peach Salsa

Mango and Chile Margaritas

Mini Mahi Mahi Tacos

THE HANG OUT

INSPIRATION Hitting the pause button on life and slowing down to savor the present moment refuels the heart like nothing else. Reminding yourself to take moments filled with casual relaxation, smiles, flow, and fresh tunes is what the *hang out* is all about. Food, friends, and beauty fall into place with hardly any effort, and witty repartee spins the dining table into cheerful laughter, and provides a comfort like no other place in the world. Stop to play on the swings and slow dance with the setting sun, as you gather the tribe for this epic board party.

STYLING TIPS Use the cooking pans as serving dishes and layer metal against metal for a strong look. With this styling, there will be little to clean up afterward, keeping the relaxed fun of the pairings flowing.

Pickled Peach Salsa

MAKES ABOUT 1 CUP

½ cup apple cider vinegar

1 teaspoon sugar

1 teaspoon sea salt

1 small red onion, finely
    diced

2 tomatillos, husks removed
    and finely diced

2 peaches, peeled and finely
    diced

1 jalapeño, seeded and
    finely diced

1 bunch fresh cilantro, finely
    chopped

Juice of 2 limes

Tortilla chips

Gently heat the vinegar, sugar, and salt in a saucepan until the sugar and salt dissolve. In a bowl or Mason jar, mix together the onion, tomatillos, peaches, jalapeño, cilantro, and lime juice. Add the pickling brine to jar. Leave to ferment for at least 1 hour.

Strain pickling liquid and serve with tortilla chips.

Mini Mahi Mahi Tacos

MAKES 8 SMALL TACOS

1 teaspoon smoked paprika

1 teaspoon chipotle powder

1 teaspoon garlic powder

1 teaspoon onion powder

1 teaspoon celery salt

1 teaspoon ground cumin

½ teaspoon black pepper

1 teaspoon dark brown
   sugar

1½ pounds mahi mahi fillets,
   cut into small pieces

1 tablespoon coconut oil

8 (6-inch) organic corn
   tortillas

½ cup thinly sliced red
   cabbage

½ cup thinly sliced green
   cabbage

½ cup grated carrots

8 lime wedges

Cilantro

Sour cream

Place spices in a dry pan and toast for a couple minutes to help meld the flavors. Remove from the heat and add the brown sugar.

Sprinkle some of the spice blend over the fish, massaging into the flesh. This blend packs a kick, so go lightly. Save any extra for next time.

Melt the oil in a large cast iron skillet over medium-high heat. Once melted, introduce the fish to the pan. Let brown on first side about 2 minutes before turning. Cook fish another 2-3 minutes on the second side until done.

Warm tortillas according to package directions.

Share fish evenly among tortillas. Top with cabbage, carrots, lime, cilantro, and a small dollop of sour cream.

Grilled Summer Squash and Spring Onions

SERVES 4

1 pound yellow summer
    squash

2 bunches spring onions

2 tablespoons olive oil

Salt and pepper, to taste

Slice the yellow squash lengthwise about ¼ inch thick. Clean and trim the spring onions. Place everything in a bowl and coat with oil and salt and pepper.

Grill on hot grill for 5 minutes per side.

Mango and Chile Margaritas

SERVES 4

2 cups frozen mango chunks

¼ cup lime juice

½ cup tequila

1 tablespoon Cointreau

1 tablespoon finely chopped
   fresh jalapeño

2 cups ice cubes

Chili power, to taste

Salt, to taste

Blend mango, lime juice, tequila, Cointreau, jalapeño, and ice cubes together in a blender. Combine chili powder and salt on a plate. Dampen the rims of glasses and dip in chili-salt mixture. Serve chilled drinks in the prepared glasses.

charcuterie

a store where pork products, as hams,
sausages, and pâtés are sold

BOARD IT UP: Charcuterie boards are filled with meats and cheeses and feel like you hit the best Italian markets for the variety and elegance of the presentation. Think sexy and casual or trying hard without trying at all when putting a charcuterie board together. You want it to look elegantly sloppy and rustically beautiful to your guests. The ingredients do all the talking on these boards and the art will be in the layout.

-Layer Pastrami Club

Calabrese Salami and Double Gloucester Cheese

Pomegranate and Orange Jam

Grilled Strawberries, Nectarines, and Apricots

Dandelion Wine

Spiced Seeds and Nuts

AFTERNOON PICNIC

INSPIRATION Envision yourself by a riverbank, lounging on warm blankets in the fresh air. The dappled light of the sun filters through the leaves of overhanging tree boughs, and a soft breeze whisks away any cares or worries. There is no place else to be, nothing else to do but be in the present moment. Highlight the freedom and relaxation of this scene with tempting bursts of flavor and fun when you dive into creating this board.

STYLING TIPS Cut the sandwich into quarters and thread onto long skewers. Use small seasonal fresh flowers for garnish. The jam pairs well with the meat and cheese.

Pomegranate and Orange Jam

MAKES 3 PINTS

3 ½ cups freshly squeezed pomegranate juice or unsweetened bottled juice

1 (1 ¾-ounce) package fruit pectin

Juice and zest of 1 orange

3 cups sugar

1 cup pomegranate seeds (from 1 large pomegranate)

In a heavy-bottom, nonreactive pan, combine the pomegranate juice, pectin, orange juice, and zest. On high heat, bring to a full boil, stirring constantly. Once really boiling, add the sugar. Keep stirring for another 2–3 minutes; once it is boiling again.

Remove from heat and skim off any pink foam. Stir in the pomegranate seeds.

Carefully, as it will be very hot, pour into 3 pint-size sterilized jam jars. Leave about ¼-inch headspace at the top and secure lids as per manufacturers directions.

Submerge the jars in a pan of water and bring to a boil. Process for 5 minutes. Carefully remove jars and allow to cool completely.

Grilled Strawberries, Nectarines, and Apricots

SERVES 4

8 strawberries, hulled and
    halved

4 apricots, pitted and halved

4 nectarines, pitted and
    halved

3 tablespoons white
    balsamic vinegar

2 tablespoons sugar

Gently place all the fruit in a bowl and mix with balsamic
vinegar. Sprinkle sugar over the fruit to lightly coat.

Place fruit cut side down on an oiled grill and grill for about
5 minutes—do not let the fruit over cook and break apart.
Serve warm.

Dandelion Wine

MAKES 1 GALLON

3 quarts dandelion blossoms

1 gallon pure water, boiling

3 pounds sugar

3 lemons, quartered

3 oranges, quartered

2 tablespoon wine yeast

Infuse the water with the dandelion petals. To do this, place all of the blossoms in a large pot and add boiling water. Leave for 48 hours.

Strain and squeeze all of the liquid out of the flowers. Discard the flowers.

In a large pot, mix the dandelion water, sugar, lemons, and oranges. Bring to a boil and keep simmering for 30 minutes. Turn off heat and let cool to tepid. Add yeast.

Cover with cheesecloth to strain and transfer to demijohn and let ferment for 2–3 weeks. Make sure the bubbling stops before bottling or you run the risk of your bottles exploding. Strain one final time before bottling.

It is important to only use the yellow petals when making dandelion wine. Any green parts of the plant make a bitter and unsatisfying brew. Many an herbalist will also recommend that you pick the blossoms early in the morning while they are still dewy.

Three-Layer Pastrami Club

SERVES 4 TO 6

¼ cup stone-ground honey mustard

12 slices whole-wheat sourdough bread, toasted

¼ cup mayonnaise

2 pounds thinly sliced pastrami

2 ripe avocados

12 slices smoked bacon, cooked

1 package arugula

Spread mustard on one side of 4 slices of bread. Spread mayonnaise on one side of 4 slices of bread. The remaining 4 slices of bread need mayonnaise on one side and mustard on the other.

Assemble the sandwich by placing toast with the mustard facing up on a plate. Next layer a generous amount of pastrami then the bread with both mayonnaise and mustard on top of that. Next layer the avocado, bacon, and arugula and top with the mayonnaise toast, mayonnaise side down.

Serve sliced in half with a pick holding it together.

Spiced Seeds and Nuts

SERVES 4

3 tablespoons butter

½ cup pecans

½ cup pine nuts

½ cup hazelnuts

½ cup walnuts

½ cup pumpkin seeds

½ cup sesame seeds

½ cup sunflower seeds

½ teaspoon cinnamon

1 teaspoon cumin

1 teaspoon paprika

½ teaspoon chili flakes

½ teaspoon salt

½ teaspoon pepper

In a medium saucepan, melt butter over medium heat. Add nuts, seeds, and all the spices. Toss to coat well and cook until lightly toasted and golden.

Serve warm or at room temperature.

FINISHING THE BOARD

Grab thinly sliced Calabrese salami, a generous chunk of Double Gloucester cheese, and your favorite crackers from the deli to serve on this board. You can also add some sliced and toasted bread.

Baked Herbed Camembert and
Brie Rounds and French Baguette

Chilled Dry French
Rosé Wine

Lavender Iced
Butter Cookies

Olive Tapenade

Herbs de Provence
Pan Roasted Chicken

FRENCH RIVIERA

INSPIRATION Cool blue waters, Edith Piaf crooning in the background, the heat of the golden sun infusing your every cell is the backdrop to this joyful board. The languid splendor of the French Riviera provides an opulent setting for classic foods. This is a refined board with simple, delicious tastes. Take yourself on French holiday without even leaving the comfort of your home.

STYLING TIPS Bring in timeless French style with bold stripes, clean white linens and an Edith Piaf playlist when styling this French inspired board.

Baked Herbed Camembert and Brie Rounds

SERVES 4 TO 6

1 wheel Camembert

1 wheel Brie

Fresh sprigs of rosemary, marjoram, and thyme

Drizzle of olive oil

1 French baguette, warmed and sliced

Preheat oven to 350 degrees F.

Score through the rind of the cheeses, both horizontally and vertically. Poke the fresh herb sprigs into the top of the cheeses along the score lines, and drizzle with olive oil. Bake for 15–20 minutes until golden and gooey. Serve while hot with warm French baguette slices.

Olive Tapenade

SERVES 4

2 cups French olives, pitted

1 tablespoon capers

2 oil-preserved anchovies

1 clove garlic, crushed

Zest and juice of 1 lemon

1 teaspoon minced fresh thyme

1 teaspoon minced fresh marjoram

1 teaspoon minced fresh parsley

2 tablespoons olive oil

Sea salt and cracked black pepper, to taste

1 French baguette, warmed and sliced

Place all of the ingredients, except salt and pepper, in a food processor and blend until it becomes a chunky paste.

Olives can be quite salty, so check before you season as it may not need any more salt. Add pepper. Serve with warm French baguette.

Pâté

16 ounces chicken livers, preferably from organic pastured chickens

½ cup chopped white onion

½ cup plus 1 tablespoon butter, divided

2 cloves garlic, chopped

3 sprigs fresh thyme

1 bay leaf

3 juniper berries

3 tablespoons brandy

1 teaspoon nutmeg

½ cup butter, melted

Flaked sea salt, to taste

Cracked black pepper, to taste

4 tablespoons melted butter, for topping

Clean any stringy, fatty parts off of the chicken livers. In a large skillet, cook onion in 1 tablespoon butter.

Once the onions have started to brown, add the chicken livers, garlic, thyme, bay leaf, juniper berries, and ½ cup butter. Cook for a couple minutes, until just browned. Don't overcook or the livers will become tough.

Add the brandy and nutmeg and cook for 1 minute more, scraping any sticky bits off of the bottom of the skillet. Remove from heat.

In a food processor, whiz the chicken liver mixture until it is smooth. Once smooth, whiz in the ½ cup melted butter and season well with salt and pepper.

Spoon into ramekins and pour the last 4 tablespoons of melted butter over the top. Allow to set until ready to serve.

Herbs de Provence Pan-Roasted Chicken

SERVES 4

2 tablespoons olive oil

2 tablespoons herbs de Provence

4 to 6 boneless, skinless chicken thighs

2 tablespoons butter

Lemon wedges

Salt and pepper, to taste

Massage olive oil and herbs de Provence into the chicken thighs.

Melt the butter in a large skillet then add the chicken. Cook on medium-low heat until chicken is browned and cooked all the way through, about 10 minutes. Add in the lemon wedges toward the end of the cooking time, and season with salt and pepper. Once cooked though, allow to rest for 5 minutes and then thinly slice and add to the board.

Iced Lavender Butter Cookies

MAKES 12 COOKIES

Cookies

2 cups all-purpose flour

¼ teaspoon salt

2 drops lavender essential oil

1 ½ teaspoons lemon zest

1 cup unsalted butter, room
   temperature

¾ cup powdered sugar

1 teaspoon vanilla extract

1 tablespoon dried lavender

1 tablespoon milk

Combine the flour, salt, essential oil, and lemon zest in a small glass bowl. Set aside.

Use a stand mixer to beat the butter and powdered sugar until smooth and creamy, 3–4 minutes. Beat in the vanilla, lavender, and milk. Slowly add in the flour mixture and mix until just combined. Form the dough into a disk shape and wrap in plastic wrap. Chill the dough for at least 1 hour.

When ready to bake, preheat oven to 325 degrees F. Line a large baking sheet with parchment paper and set aside.

On a lightly floured surface, roll out the dough into a ¼-inch-thick circle. Cut into rounds using a lightly floured cookie cutter. Place cookies on the prepared baking sheet and bake for 10–12 minutes, or until cookies are very lightly browned around the edges. Remove cookies from baking sheet and cool completely on a wire rack.

Glaze

2 cups powdered sugar

¼ to ⅓ cup milk

¼ cup dried lavender, for
   decorating

Combine powdered sugar
and milk in a small bowl.
Stir until a thick glaze forms.
Dip cookies into the glaze.
Add the dried lavender as
decoration on each cookie
before the glaze dries.

FINISHING THE BOARD

Finish the board with a
chilled dry French rosé wine.

Sangria

Pan-Roasted Peppers

Smoked Paprika Almonds

Spanish Mini Churros
and Melted Chocolate

Spanish Chorizo

Patatas Bravas with Spicy Tomato Sauce

SPANISH TAPAS

INSPIRATION An evening on the Mediterranean with the sun setting and a soft ocean breeze upon your skin is a dreamy place to visit in your mind when designing this tapas board. The combination of salty and spicy flavors will keep you wanting for more of these sexy Spanish bites.

STYLING TIPS With this board, you want to keep your styling simple and rustic. Use various small dipping bowls for the sauces to give your board texture and variation of proportions. Think Spain when you are pulling this board together and enjoy a sweet night with friends and good food.

Smoked Paprika Almonds

SERVES 4

2 cups raw almonds

1 tablespoon sea salt

½ teaspoon smoked sweet hot paprika

½ teaspoon dried mustard powder

1 tablespoon extra virgin olive oil

Preheat oven to 400 degrees F.

Spread the almonds onto an ungreased baking sheet and toast in the oven for 8–10 minutes, shifting now and again, until almonds are golden brown.

While the nuts are toasting, combine the sea salt, paprika, and mustard in a mortar and pestle and mix together well.

Remove the almonds from the oven and drizzle them with olive oil and toss to combine. Sprinkle with the paprika mixture and mix a second time. Add to a rustic container with parchment paper.

Spanish Chorizo

SERVES 4

1 pound Spanish chorizo

1 teaspoon olive oil

Salt and pepper, to taste

Slice the chorizo into ¼-inch slices. Heat oil in a skillet and fry the chorizo until crisp. Season with salt and pepper. Serve warm.

Patatas Bravas with Spicy Tomato Sauce

SERVES 4

2 pounds Yukon Gold potatoes, cut into bite-size pieces

Sea salt, to taste

2 tablespoons olive oil, divided

½ yellow onion, diced

3 cloves garlic, minced

½ teaspoon paprika

Pinch of cayenne pepper

1 teaspoon garlic powder plus more for potatoes

1 (6-ounce) can tomato paste

2 to 3 teaspoons hot sauce

1½ cups water

I bunch fresh parsley, chopped

Parmesan cheese

Preheat oven to 450 degrees F.

Place the potatoes on a baking sheet and sprinkle with salt and 1 tablespoon olive oil. Toss to coat. Bake for 20–25 minutes, or until golden brown and cooked through, stirring a couple of times.

While the potatoes are baking, prepare the spicy tomato sauce. In a medium saucepan, heat remaining olive oil over medium-low heat. Add onion, garlic, and a pinch of salt and stir.

Add paprika, cayenne, and garlic powder and mix together. Stir in tomato paste, hot sauce, and water. Cook until simmering then turn down the heat. Adjust spices to taste, adding more if needed.

Remove potatoes from oven and sprinkle with more garlic powder or salt if needed. Sprinkle the potatoes with fresh parsley, the spicy tomato sauce, and a bit of Parmesan cheese

Pan-Roasted Peppers

SERVES 4

1 tablespoon extra virgin olive
    oil

1 pound Padrón peppers, or
    use any mild green pepper

1 tablespoon sea salt

½ teaspoon chili flakes

Heat oil in a skillet.

Toss the peppers, salt, and chili flakes into the skillet. Keep turning until well colored and the skin is crackling. Serve warm.

Spanish Mini Churros and Melted Chocolate

SERVES 4

Vegetable oil

½ cup milk

½ cup water

3 tablespoons butter, diced

¼ teaspoon salt

2 teaspoons sugar

½ teaspoon vanilla extract

1 cup all-purpose flour

Cinnamon Sugar Coating

½ cup sugar

2 teaspoons ground cinnamon

Pinch of cardamom

Dark Chocolate Dip

8 ounces bittersweet chocolate

In a large saucepan, heat approximately 2 inches of oil over medium heat to 360 degrees F. Use a candy thermometer to monitor the temperature.

In a separate saucepan, heat together the milk, water, butter, salt, and sugar and bring mixture just to a slow boil. Once it reaches a boil, remove from heat and immediately stir in vanilla and flour. Make sure to get your mixture smooth, without bubbles.

Let cool to a warm temperature and transfer the dough to a piping bag. This will make it easier to control the size of each churro as you pipe the dough into the oil. Do not put too many churros into the oil at one time, as you do not want them to stick together.

Fry churros until light golden brown, and then scoop out of the oil and place on a paper towel to dry.

Cinnamon Sugar Coating

In a small bowl, mix together the sugar, cinnamon, and cardamom and roll each churro in the sugar mixture.

Dark Chocolate Dip

In a double boiler, or a bowl over a pot of boiling water, melt the dark chocolate and serve warm as a dipping sauce for the churros.

Sangria

SERVES 4

1 bottle Spanish red wine

¼ cup orange juice

1 orange, thinly sliced

1 lemon, thinly sliced

1 lime, thinly sliced

1 apple, thinly sliced

¼ cup brandy

2 tablespoons brown sugar

Sparkling water or Prosecco,
  optional

Mix wine, juice, fruit, and brandy together in a large serving pitcher. Add lots of ice. When you pour into glasses, top with sparkling water or Prosecco if you like.

Sage-Infused Homemade Ricotta Cheese

Italian Salami and Prosciutto

Various Olives and Cornichons

Rosemary-Infused Olive Oil

Crisp Red Grapes

Focaccia

Roasted Figs with Balsamic Glaze

CLASSIC ITALIAN

INSPIRATION From the sun-drenched shores of the Mediterranean Sea to the ancient olive groves of the countryside, Italy beckons with a siren song of ruins, history, and passion. It is a country of artists, dreamers, and lovers. The food is renowned for its bright flavors, nuanced with intensity and depth.

STYLING TIPS The wonderful thing about charcuterie boards is that they can be thrown together easily. All you need is a board, meat, fruit, and cheese. Vintage stores are a great place to find Italian glass for your olive oil as it will look gorgeous out on display.

Roasted Figs with Balsamic Glaze

SERVES 4

Butter

2 pounds fresh figs, cleaned and halved

¼ cup balsamic vinegar

2 tablespoons local honey

1 tablespoon brown sugar

1 tablespoon orange zest

Squeeze of orange juice

Preheat oven to 400 degrees F. Thoroughly butter a baking dish large enough to hold the figs. Arrange the figs in the dish cut side down.

Whisk together the rest of the ingredients and pour over figs.

Roast for about 20 minutes until the figs are caramelized. Be careful not burn them. Serve warm.

Sage-Infused Homemade Ricotta Cheese

SERVES 4

4 cups whole organic milk

1 cup organic cream

1 sprig fresh sage, 4 to 5 leaves

½ teaspoon salt

2 tablespoons lemon juice

1 tablespoon white wine vinegar

Salt and pepper, to taste

Honey

Olive oil

Sage leaves

Combine milk, cream, sage, and salt in a nonreactive pan. Over high heat, bring mixture to a boil. Turn down heat and add lemon juice and vinegar. Simmer for another couple minutes until you see curds begin to form. Pour the mixture into a strainer lined with 2 layers of damp cheesecloth and set over a bowl.

Let the liquid drain for at least 45 minutes. Check on it every so often to pour off any liquid that runs off. The longer you leave it, the firmer the ricotta will be.

Store the ricotta in the refrigerator until you're ready to use it. Season with salt and pepper before serving and drizzle with honey and olive oil. Garnish with sage leaves.

Focaccia

2 ½ cups all-purpose flour

1 teaspoon salt

¼ cup plus 2 tablespoon olive oil, divided

1 (¼-ounce) packet active dry yeast

1 teaspoon sugar

1 cup tepid water

Flaked sea salt, to taste

Preheat oven to 425 degrees F. Mix together flour, salt, and 2 tablespoons olive oil in a large mixing bowl.

Mix the yeast, sugar, and water together and let bloom. Once the yeast mixture is foamy and active, add to the flour mixture. Stir well with a spoon until the dough begins to form and stick together.

Turn the dough out onto lightly floured surface and knead until smooth and elastic. This can take a few minutes, so be patient and keep working the dough with your hands, pulling, stretching, and reforming into a ball, repeating over and over again until it is smooth and stretchy.

Place the dough in a bowl and cover with a damp towel to rise—at least 30 minutes. Placing in a warm spot can help.

Punch the dough down and place on greased baking sheet. Pat dough into ½-inch-thick rectangle shape. Make indentations in the dough about ½ inch apart using your fingers or knuckles. Mark the dough all over with a fork and brush with the remaining olive oil. Sprinkle with flaked sea salt. Bake for 15 minutes until the bottom is brown and cooked. Slice to serve.

Rosemary-Infused Olive Oil

MAKES 2 CUPS

3 fresh sprigs rosemary

3 peppercorns

1 (16-ounce) bottle extra
   virgin olive oil

Salt and pepper, to taste

Place rosemary and peppercorns in the olive oil bottle. Season with salt and pepper. Let marinate for 48 hours. Use within 1–2 months.

FINISHING THE BOARD

Get good-quality prosciutto and salami from your local Italian delicatessen. Serve everything with luscious crisp, red grapes, assorted olives, cornichons, and a sweet Prosecco.

lush

luxuriant; succulent; tender and juicy

BOARD IT UP: Lush boards are decadent and ooey-gooey. They are meant to be luxurious and succulent and should have sinful foods that melt in your mouth. Lush boards have to be beautiful, sexy, and filled with color and temptation. So don't hold back on these delicious combinations.

Spiced
Dark Chocolate
Truffles

Roasted Rainbow Carrots

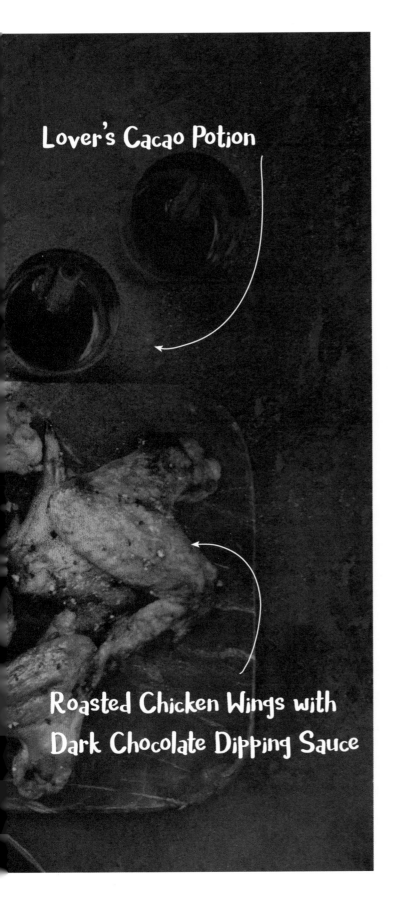

Lover's Cacao Potion

Roasted Chicken Wings with
Dark Chocolate Dipping Sauce

TEMPTATION

INSPIRATION This is a meal made in devotion to your beloved. Layer divine passion into each ingredient. Prepare each selection as a lover goes in for a deep kiss, with your whole heart. As you imbue each ingredient with sweet loving intention, the potent gift of the whole offering increases. No matter who your beloved is—yourself or someone else, make this a true present of the heart.

STYLING TIPS Romance is a real art. Take time to notice the small details that speak to your beloved and incorporate those into the presentation. Maybe add a picture of the two of you to your board, or an actual small gift of massage oil for a second dessert later on in the evening. Whatever you choose, make sure to have drippy love on your mind and maybe hand feeding!

Roasted Chicken Wings with Dark Chocolate Dipping Sauce

SERVES 2

1 pound chicken wings

Salt and pepper, to taste

2 tablespoons butter

½ cup thinly sliced onion

¼ cup balsamic vinegar

2 tablespoons brown sugar

2 ounces dark chocolate

½ teaspoon cinnamon

½ teaspoon allspice

1 clove garlic, crushed

1 cup chicken stock

Preheat oven to 375 degrees F and season the chicken wings with salt and pepper.

Melt butter in a skillet over medium-high heat. Once hot and bubbling, add chicken and allow to brown for about 5 minutes. Flip the chicken and cook for another couple minutes. Remove from the skillet, place into an ovenproof dish, and put in the oven for about 20 minutes, until cooked through.

Once chicken is in the oven, turn the heat down to medium-low and add the onion to the skillet and slowly cook for 5–10 minutes. Add the rest of the ingredients and let the sauce reduce while the chicken finishes cooking.

When the chicken is ready, remove from oven and let rest for 5–10 minutes. Pour the sauce into a serving dish and serve on the side with the roasted chicken wings.

Roasted Rainbow Carrots

SERVES 2

½ pound rainbow carrots

2 tablespoons olive oil

½ teaspoon salt

½ teaspoon pepper

Preheat oven to 375 degrees F. Wash and peel the carrots. Trim any greens, leaving about ½-inch greens at the end. Massage the carrots with the olive oil and then season with salt and pepper.

Place on baking sheet in single layer and roast for 20–30 minutes, stirring occasionally to prevent sticking.

Lover's Cacao Potion

SERVES 2

1 ½ cups dark chocolate pieces

½ teaspoon nutmeg

½ teaspoon chili powder

½ teaspoon cinnamon

1 cup hot water

Rose petals

Melt the chocolate in a pan over very low heat, stirring constantly. Once melted, add in the spices. Whisk in the water until it is a thick, drinkable consistency.

Serve warm in cups garnished with rose petals.

Spiced Dark Chocolate Truffles

MAKES 12 TO 24 TRUFFLES

½ cup organic whole cream

1 vanilla bean, split open

½ teaspoon cinnamon

1 teaspoon organic rose petals

1 cup dark chocolate pieces, 62 percent cacao or higher

Cocoa powder

Powdered rose petals

Place the cream, vanilla bean, cinnamon, and rose petals in a saucepan and bring to simmer. Do not boil. Let simmer for at least 15 minutes to infuse the flavors.

Place the chocolate in a separate bowl. Strain the infused cream into the bowl with the chocolate and stir until the chocolate has melted and combined into the milk. This is now ganache. Refrigerate for 2 hours.

Once cool, use a small melon baller or teaspoon to scoop out the chocolate. Form into balls and place on a baking sheet lined with parchment paper. Chill overnight.

Roll truffles in cocoa powder and sprinkle with powdered rose petals. Keep chilled until ready to use.

Baked Brie Pastry, Fig Jam, and Fresh Thyme with Baguette Slices

Red Grapes and Dark Chocolate

Prosciutto-Wrapped Asparagus

Salami and Cheeses

JUST SINFUL

INSPIRATION This is an ooey, gooey sinful board that reminds you of decadence and all the foods that comfort the soul. It's a whole body yes to this cheesy plate, and it will delight your guests with flavors of salty sweetness.

STYLING TIPS This board should reflect a light mood and atmosphere. Gather the asparagus spears into a stylish glass for serving, and encourage finger licking with these delectable treats.

Served w/ lentil soup

Baked Brie Pastry, Fig Jam, and Fresh Thyme with Baguette Slices

SERVES 4

1 egg

1 can crescent rolls (ready-to-bake dough)

1 round Brie cheese *small*

2 tablespoons fig jam

2 sprigs fresh thyme

1 French baguette, warmed and sliced

Preheat oven to 350 degrees F. Whisk egg in a small bowl and set aside.

Open the can of ready-made crescent roll dough and gently tear it apart to make a square, reserving the rest to lay on top of the Brie after its folded up. Lay the dough on a Silpat or parchment paper.

Place the Brie in the center of the dough and top with the jam and thyme sprigs.

Lay the extra piece of dough over top of the Brie and then fold up the rest of the dough around the Brie like you are wrapping a present. Brush the dough with the egg. Bake for approximately 30 minutes, or until browned. Serve warm, topped with fresh thyme and baguette slices.

pretty good

Prosciutto-Wrapped Asparagus

SERVES 4

16 spears asparagus

16 pieces prosciutto

Olive oil

Salt and pepper, to taste

Preheat oven to 350 degrees F. Wash the asparagus and break off woody ends.

Wrap 1 piece of prosciutto around each spear, and place on baking sheet. Drizzle with olive oil and season with salt and pepper. Roast for about 20 minutes, or until asparagus is cooked and prosciutto is crispy.

FINISHING THE BOARD

Add generous portions of seasonal grapes, dark chocolate pieces, and a selection of local cheeses and salami to the board.

OK. Smaller prosciutto pieces

Spiced Espresso Shots

Fried Capers

Chocolate-Swirl
Mini Meringues

Blue Cheese and
Chèvre Arugula Salad

Sliced Filet Mignon

Brown Buttered
Scallops

SURF AND TURF

INSPIRATION You can have it all. This decadent and divine board is the reward for your life's journey. Each step on your path has led you to this moment. You have permission to really shine your light and give this gift of sumptuous opulence to yourself. Pull out all the stops and prepare this meal for you and a beloved—although it is perfectly acceptable not to share!

STYLING TIPS Let nature hold up the beauty of this meal. Serve it on dark slate with antique cutlery. Wear your finest clothes. And do it all on Wednesday. Just because.

Sliced Filet Mignon

SERVES 2

1 (6- to 8-ounce) filet mignon

Salt, to taste

1 tablespoon coarsely
    ground peppercorns

1 tablespoon olive oil

¼ cup balsamic vinegar

1 tablespoon brown sugar

Preheat oven to 420 degrees F and season steak with salt. Sprinkle peppercorns on a plate and press steak into them. Repeat on the other side of the steak.

Heat olive oil in an ovenproof skillet over high heat. Add steak and sear for 2 minutes per side. Also sear the sides of the steak, for about 30 seconds, to seal in all the juices.

Put the steak in the oven for about 4–5 minutes for medium-rare. Remove steak and cover in foil to rest for 5–10 minutes.

Make a balsamic reduction by pouring the balsamic vinegar and brown sugar into a small pan over medium heat. Reduce by half or until thick and syrupy. Do not burn.

take it off heat

Thinly slice the steak against the grain. Serve on top of the Blue Cheese and Chèvre Arugula Salad page 106.

good

Brown Buttered Scallops

SERVES 2

1 tablespoon olive oil

6 king scallops

Pinch each of salt and
   pepper

2 tablespoons butter, cubed

1 tablespoon lemon juice

1 tablespoon flat-leaf
   parsley, chopped

Heat oil in skillet over high heat. Pat dry scallops and season with salt and pepper. Cook scallops for 2 minutes undisturbed. Turn scallops and add butter to pan. Continue cooking for 2 minutes, spooning the butter over the scallops.

When the scallops are cooked and the butter is brown and starting to smell nutty, remove from heat, add lemon juice, and parsley then serve.

good

Blue Cheese and Chèvre Arugula Salad

No Blue

SERVES 2

2 cups arugula

½ cup chèvre (soft goat's
   cheese)

½ cup crumbled blue cheese

Pinch of salt

Place arugula on plate and layer with dollops of chèvre and blue cheese. Sprinkle with salt and top with Sliced Filet Mignon (page 104) and Brown Buttered Scallops.

Fried Capers

good

GARNISH

1 tablespoon capers

½ cup vegetable oil

Heat oil in small pan to about 375 degrees F. Rinse capers in a sieve then pat dry between paper towels.

Deep fry capers in oil for 30–40 seconds until golden. Remove with slotted spoon and drain on paper towels. These are a tasty addition to the Blue Cheese and Chèvre Arugula Salad.

Spiced Espresso Shots

SERVES 2

2 shots espresso

½ teaspoon cinnamon syrup

Make the espresso as directed by your coffee machine. Finish each with ¼ teaspoon of cinnamon syrup.

Chocolate-Swirl Mini Meringues

Meringues

4 large egg whites

⅛ teaspoon salt

1 cup sugar

2 teaspoons cornstarch

1 teaspoon vanilla extract

1 teaspoon white wine
    vinegar

Chocolate

8 ounces chocolate, melted
    and cooled

Preheat oven to 350 degrees F.

Using a stand mixer with a whisk attachment, whisk the egg whites and salt together until they form peaks that hold their shape. Keep slowly whisking while you add in the sugar a little at a time. Whisk until the egg whites transform into stiff, glossy peaks of meringue. Turn off mixer and add cornstarch, vanilla, and vinegar and gently whisk to just combine. You don't want to knock all the air out of the egg whites.

Drizzle some of the chocolate on top of the meringue—no need to mix in. Scoop spoonfuls of this chocolaty, floaty goodness onto baking sheets lined with parchment paper. Drizzle more chocolate on top of the meringue as you continue scooping. When all of the chocolate and meringue has been scooped, place the baking sheets into the oven and turn the heat down to 300 degrees F and bake for 30 minutes.

Turn the oven off but leave the meringues in the oven for another 20–30 minutes. They are ready when the meringues easily lift off of the parchment paper. Remove and let cool. Keeps well stored in an airtight container.

Mini Cheesecake Crème Brûlée with Fig Jam Drip

Red Wine

Red Velvet Mini Donuts with Swirl Icing

Red Wine Ice Cream with Fresh Blackberries and Plums

BAD DAY TONIC

INSPIRATION Have you ever had a just a bad day and all you want are some comfort treats to soothe the blues a bit? While that may not be the answer to your woes, this board will help bring your energy back up to neutral while tantalizing your taste buds along the way.

STYLING TIPS This is a sophisticated moment for you and your board styling. Think deep reds and a sultry night with a good romance novel to inspire you to make this board as beautiful as it can be. Dive deep to reflect a moody presentation that would cheer up your best friend on a hard night.

Mini Cheesecake Crème Brûlée with Fig Jam Drip

12 full-size graham crackers

¼ cup unsalted butter, melted

16 ounces cream cheese, softened and room temperature

¼ cup sour cream, room temperature

¾ cup sugar

2 large eggs, room temperature

1 large egg yolk, room temperature

1 vanilla bean, split and scraped

¼ teaspoon fine sea salt

Sugar, as needed to brûlée tops

Edible flowers

Preheat oven to 325 degrees F. Use a muffin pan to make the mini crème brûlée, and use coconut oil spray for the bottoms of the cups so the cakes will not stick.

In a food processor, pulse together graham crackers until finely ground. Combine the ground graham crackers with the butter and thoroughly combine.

Using a tablespoon, scoop the graham cracker mixture into the bottom of each muffin cup and firmly pack. Set aside to prepare the cream cheese filling.

In a stand mixer, combine the cream cheese, sour cream, and sugar. Combine until smooth then slowly add in the eggs and yolk, one at a time, and mix until smooth. Add in the vanilla bean seeds and salt and mix once more.

Evenly divide the cream cheese filling into the muffin cups, and bake for 15–19 minutes, until lightly browned. Remove from the oven and let cool to room temperature.

Place the mini cheesecakes into the refrigerator and chill for 20–30 minutes. Remove the cakes from the muffin cups and top each one with a sprinkle of sugar. Brûlée with a kitchen torch and serve with a drizzle of Fig Jam Drip and an edible flower or two.

Fig Jam Drip

3 tablespoons fig jam (sold
    in the jam section at your
    local health food store)

⅓ stick butter

In a small saucepan, melt
the fig jam and the but-
ter together. The jam will
become a drippy sauce
within 2–3 minutes. Drizzle it
over the cooled cheesecakes
and serve on a lush board.

Red Velvet Mini Donuts with Swirl Icing

Donuts

Coconut spray oil

1 cup buttermilk

1 tablespoon vanilla extract

3 tablespoons beet powder

1 cup sugar

1 cup all-purpose flour

¼ cup cocoa powder

½ teaspoon baking powder

½ teaspoon baking soda

½ teaspoon sea salt

Preheat oven to 350 degrees F. Prepare a mini donut pan with coconut spray oil.

In a large bowl, combine buttermilk and vanilla. After well mixed, add in the beet powder and sugar.

In another bowl, mix the flour, cocoa powder, baking powder, baking soda, and salt together until thoroughly combined.

Carefully fill each donut cup ⅔ full with the batter. Bake for 7–8 minutes. Remove donuts from oven and let cool for 5 minutes in the pan. Remove from pan and cool completely before icing.

To ice the donuts, hold each one upside down and dip it into the icing. Hold it above the bowl to let the donuts drip any extra icing before flipping right side up.

Red Swirl Icing

2 cups powdered sugar

2 teaspoons vanilla extract

5 tablespoons milk

7 drops natural red food coloring

Mix together the powdered sugar, vanilla, and milk. Drop the food coloring into the mixture in a line of 7 dots. Do not mix. Take a toothpick and drag slowly through the dots of color, creating swirl patterns. Dip your donuts into the swirls.

Red Wine Ice Cream with Fresh Blackberries and Plums

1 bottle red wine

⅓ cup packed brown sugar

⅓ cup agave

1 lemon, juiced

2 cups heavy whipping cream

1 vanilla bean

4 egg yolks

1 cup half-and-half

Fresh blackberries

Fresh plums

In a large saucepan on low heat, bring the wine to a simmer and reduce to 1 cup. This can take a while, up to an hour, so be sure to keep checking as it simmers. Set aside for later.

In a saucepan on medium heat, whisk together brown sugar, agave, lemon juice, and cream. Slice the vanilla bean in half, scrape seeds, and add both seeds and bean to the cream mixture, stirring constantly until steaming, but not boiling.

As the cream is cooking, beat the eggs in a stand mixer until light and fluffy. Very slowly to prevent curdling, add the cream mixture to the yolks. Return the yolk mixture back to the saucepan and stir on medium heat until it thickens.

Pour the half-and-half through a strainer into a large bowl and then pour the egg cream mixture through the strainer into the same bowl. Mix together then add in the reduced red wine. Refrigerate this mixture for several hours.

Take the mixture out of the refrigerator and process in an ice cream maker according to manufacturer instructions. Serve the ice cream with blackberries and sliced plums.

FINISHING THE BOARD

Serve up the board with a juicy Pinot Noir or dark and moody Zinfandel.

RUSTIC
BOARDS

rustic

of, relating to, or living in the country, as distinguished from towns or cities; rural

BOARD IT UP: Rustic boards are full of comfort foods and old-school re-interpretations. They are meant for family gatherings outside on a warm summer night or surprise vintage gatherings with a local banjo band playing in the background. They should be fresh picked, fun, and tasty with the charm of a renovated barn in the background to pump up the ambience.

Mini Mac 'n' Cheese Cups

Root Beer-Braised
Barbecue Ribs

Cinnamon-Apple Hand Pies

Fresh Lemon, Lime, and Mint Soda

SITTIN' ON THE PORCH

INSPIRATION To get ready to dive into the energy of this board, try envisioning children playing in sprinklers on a hot summer day, an ice-cold drink in your hands, and the luxury of rest and time to be completely present. This is slow food for precious moments, savored in the delectable exhalation of life. You want to sit back in that rocking chair and tune into what makes your heart sing as you unfold the feeling behind creating this board of pure southern comfort foods. This is feel-good food, and feel-good living that elevates the mundane to the extraordinary through presence and intention.

STYLING TIPS These ribs are so tender they have a tendency to melt apart. Serve them with finger bowls of lemon water to save on the napkins and add a southern charm to the presentation. The pie pops can be held in a tin can filled with sand to keep them upright or even on parchment paper. You may consider several old bottles for the soda and small tins for the mac 'n' cheese. Have fun with this relaxed board.

Root Beer-Braised Barbecue Ribs

SERVES 2 TO 4

1 pound short ribs

Salt and pepper, to taste

1 tablespoon olive oil

1 onion, chopped

1 carrot, chopped

1 stalk celery, chopped

2 cloves garlic, crushed

1 small sprig rosemary

2 sprigs thyme

½ teaspoon ground cumin

1 cup beef broth

3 tablespoons tomato paste

1 tablespoon molasses

1 (12-ounce) bottle root beer

Preheat oven to 250 degrees F. Season ribs with salt and pepper. Heat olive oil in a Dutch oven and brown the ribs on all sides. Remove ribs and set aside.

Add onion, carrot, celery, and garlic to the Dutch oven and cook for a few minutes until softened. Add rosemary, thyme, and cumin and stir well.

Return ribs to Dutch oven and pour in broth; add tomato paste, molasses, and root beer. Cover and place in oven for 3 hours, or until ribs are very tender.

Carefully remove ribs, strain liquid, and discard solids. Skim any fat from liquid then reduce by half to make a sauce. Drizzle sauce over ribs.

Fresh Lemon, Lime, and Mint Soda

SERVES 4

1 bunch fresh mint

4 lime wedges

4 lemon wedges

4 tablespoons brown sugar

1 (750-ml) bottle soda water

Ice

In each of 4 glasses divide the mint, limes, lemons, and brown sugar. Muddle together and then top with soda water and ice.

Mini Mac 'n' Cheese Cups

Serves 6

1 cup macaroni noodles

¼ cup butter, plus extra for greasing pan

¼ cup all-purpose flour

2 cups milk

Salt and pepper, to taste

¼ teaspoon nutmeg

2 cups grated Gruyère cheese

1 cup grated sharp cheddar cheese

1 tablespoon melted butter

½ cup breadcrumbs

Preheat oven to 375 degrees F and cook macaroni according to package directions.

Melt ¼ cup butter in a large saucepan and stir in flour to make a roux. Gradually add milk and stir until thick and smooth.

Remove from heat, season with a pinch of salt and pepper, and add the nutmeg. Combine the cheeses, set aside ¼ cup of the mix, and stir the rest into the white sauce. Add cooked macaroni and stir well.

Grease a muffin pan with butter; then evenly divide the macaroni mixture between the muffin pan cups.

In a small bowl, combine the melted butter with the breadcrumbs and mix in the remaining cheese. Evenly divide the breadcrumb mixture over the tops of the macaroni cups. Bake for 20 minutes, or until browned on top.

Cinnamon-Apple Hand Pies

MAKES 10 HAND PIES

2 cups Granny Smith apples, peeled, cored, and diced

1 tablespoon lemon juice

¼ cup packed brown sugar

1 teaspoon cinnamon

½ teaspoon ground ginger

¼ teaspoon ground cloves

1 tablespoon cornstarch

1 (15–ounce) package ready-roll pie dough

1 egg, lightly beaten

Preheat oven to 375 degrees F.

Combine the apples, lemon juice, brown sugar, cinnamon, ginger, cloves, and cornstarch in a large saucepan and simmer until fruit is soft and sticky. About 5 minutes.

On a lightly floured surface, unroll the pie crusts one at a time. Using a 3-inch cookie cutter, cut out 10 circles from each crust.

Arrange the first 10 circles on a baking sheet. Scoop a small tablespoon of the apple mixture onto the center of each circle. Lightly coat the edges of the circles with a little of the egg and place another pastry round on top. Use a fork to crimp edges together and make sure they are tightly sealed. Score a decorative pattern on the tops of the pies for steam vents, and brush with a little bit of the egg. Bake for 15–20 minutes, and let cool completely before moving to a serving dish.

Cracked Crab Legs and Melted Herbed Butter

Blackberry Whiskey Lemonade

Peel-and-Eat Shrimp with Zesty Cocktail Sauce and Garlic Butter

Mini Herb-Roasted Corn on the Cob

BY THE WATERFRONT

INSPIRATION The smell of salt in the air and the soft caress of the sea breeze in your hair leaves you humming with the song of the ocean in your every cell. This tingle is the inspiration for this presentation. Every board presentation creates a feeling within us, and this one has the charm of New England written all over it. Your food should reflect the whispered secrets of the waterfront. On this one, be prepared to get messy and dig into the gifts of the ocean.

STYLING TIPS Newspaper makes a great backdrop to this board party and doubles as an easy way to clean up the shells. Don't forget to include some found seashells as decoration. Lemons are a natural complement to the brine; an abundance in a bowl will look great and be functional.

Cracked Crab Legs and Melted Herbed Butter

2 pounds king crab legs

Water

3 lemon slices

1 cup salted butter

2 tablespoons chopped fresh parsley

1 tablespoon chopped fresh thyme

1 clove garlic, crushed

Salt and pepper, to taste

King crab legs are cooked on the boat and flash frozen to preserve the flavor. All you need to do is reheat them. Let them thaw overnight in your refrigerator.

In a large stockpot, place a steaming basket, water, and the lemon slices. Once boiling, add the crab legs and cover. They are ready when they smell delicious, usually about 5–8 minutes.

Carefully remove the crab legs from pot and allow to cool enough to handle. Then, using kitchen shears, cut along the edges to crack open.

To make the herbed butter, slowly melt the butter in a small pan over medium-low heat. Once melted, add the herbs and garlic and simmer for 3 minutes on low; do not burn or boil. Season with salt and pepper. Serve the butter warm with the crab legs.

Mini Herb-Roasted Corn on the Cob

SERVES 4

¼ cup butter

1 teaspoon dried rosemary

1 teaspoon dried thyme

½ teaspoon lime zest

½ teaspoon salt

½ teaspoon cracked black
   pepper

4 small cobs of corn

Preheat oven to 400 degrees F.

Melt the butter in a small saucepan and then stir in the
rosemary, thyme, lime zest, salt and pepper.

Place the corn in an ovenproof baking dish. Baste the corn
with the herb butter and roast in oven for 30–40 minutes.
Turn and baste the corn several times as it roasts. When
finished, remove from oven and baste again. Let cool
enough to handle and then serve.

Peel-and-Eat Shrimp with Zesty Cocktail Sauce and Garlic Butter

SERVES 2

1 pound split shell and deveined raw shrimp

1 cup water

1 cup white wine

2 tablespoons butter

1 tablespoon Old Bay seasoning

4 lemon wedges

Zesty Cocktail Sauce

½ cup ketchup

¼ cup chipotle chili sauce

2 tablespoons hot horseradish

2 tablespoons lemon juice

1 teaspoon Worcestershire sauce

Place shrimp, water, and wine in a pot and bring to a boil. Cook shrimp until pink and opaque, about 4–5 minutes. Drain. Toss the shrimp with the butter and Old Bay seasoning. Serve with the lemon wedges, Zesty Cocktail Sauce and Garlic Butter.

Zesty Cocktail Sauce

Mix all the ingredients together in a small bowl. Check for seasoning and adjust to taste. Chill for 15 minutes before serving.

Garlic Butter

¼ cup butter

3 tablespoons chopped garlic

1 tablespoon chopped flat-leaf
parsley

Salt and pepper, to taste

Melt the butter in a small saucepan. Add garlic and parsley.
Season with salt and pepper
and stir to combine. Serve warm.

Blackberry Whiskey Lemonade

SERVES 2

Blackberry Syrup

1 pint fresh blackberries

¼ cup packed brown sugar

¼ cup water

4 fresh sage leaves

Whiskey Lemonade

4 ounces whiskey

4 ounces fresh-squeezed
   lemon juice

4 ounces Blackberry Syrup

Ice

Fresh sage leaves

Lemon twists

Fresh blackberries

Blackberry Syrup

Place all the ingredients into a saucepan and warm on medium-low heat until the juice is released. Simmer for about 20 minutes then turn off heat and strain, squeezing out all the syrup from the pulp. Discard the solids.

Let the syrup cool completely before making the drink.

Whiskey Lemonade

Combine the whiskey, lemon juice, and syrup in a cocktail shaker with ice and give it a good shake. Pour into 2 tumblers over additional ice and garnish with the sage leaves, lemon twists, and blackberries.

Roasted Pumpkin and Onion Skewers

Three Sisters Chili

Toasted Marshmallow S'mores

Pom Pom Juice

HARVEST MOON

INSPIRATION The nights begin to grow long, the seductive twilight calls with velveteen hues of mystery. Smokey bonfires, misty woods, and a little moonlight magic set the stage for the evening's festivities. This board is luscious and full of renaissance romance.

STYLING TIPS This is the season of bounty and harvest; celebrate by sharing your abundance. Decorate this board with gratitude notes, harvest colors, and old-school vessels such as silver, metal, and wood. Skewer the marshmallows on small sticks for roasting and serving.

Roasted Pumpkin and Onion Skewers

SERVES 4

1 small pie pumpkin, peeled
 and cut into 1-inch chunks

2 yellow onions, quartered

Extra virgin olive oil

Sea salt and pepper, to taste

Massage the pumpkin chunks and onions with the oil. Thread onto skewers, alternating pumpkin chunks and onions. Sprinkle liberally with salt and pepper. If you use wooden skewers make sure to soak them for at least an hour before using.

Grill the skewers over medium-high heat for about 20 minutes, until the pumpkin is cooked and the onions are mellow and golden. Give another sprinkle with salt and enjoy.

Three Sisters Chili

SERVES 4

1 pound ground beef

1 cup chopped pumpkin

1 cup pinto beans

1 cup kidney beans

1 cup corn kernels

1 (7-ounce) can chipotle
    peppers in adobo

1 small yellow onion, chopped

2 tablespoons maple syrup

1 tablespoon blackstrap
    molasses

1 tablespoon apple cider
    vinegar

¼ cup coconut sugar

1 teaspoon celery seed

1 cinnamon stick

1 teaspoon cumin powder

1 teaspoon garlic powder

1 teaspoon coriander powder

1 (16-ounce) can tomatoes in
    sauce

Grated cheese, of choice

Sour cream

Brown the beef in a large pot. Add the rest of the ingredients, except for the cheese and sour cream, and simmer for about 60 minutes, until everything is well cooked and the flavors meld together. Serve warm with cheese and sour cream.

Toasted Marshmallow S'mores

MAKES 12 S'MORES

12 marshmallows

24 half-size graham crackers

2 bars good-quality dark
  chocolate, each broken
  into 6 pieces

Begin by having all your ingredients close at hand. Toast the marshmallows on a stick over a fire or the barbecue. Once warm, use a cracker to push the hot marshmallow onto a piece of cracker with chocolate on top. Top with another cracker, making a marshmallow and chocolate sandwich.

Pom Pom Juice

SERVES 4

1 (32-ounce) jar pomegranate
  juice

¼ cup maple syrup

1 tablespoon sliced ginger

1 cinnamon stick

7 allspice berries

Ginger ale

Combine the juice, syrup, ginger, cinnamon, and allspice in a large saucepan and simmer until it has reduced by half. Strain to remove the solids. Divide the liquid between 4 glasses and top with ginger ale.

Homemade
Concord Grape Juice

Roasted
Mixed Vegetables

ry Galette with
lla Bean Whipped Cream

Bratwurst Sausage with
Stone-Ground Mustard

BANJO NIGHT

INSPIRATION The smell of pies on the windowsill with berry sauce dripping over the edge, backyard banjo music, Mason jar candlelight, and the sweet laughter of friends and family are the inspirations for this homespun board. This is a casual gathering lit by the glow of the setting sun.

STYLING TIPS This comfort food requires an easy-going grace to get it just right. Serve the grape juice in Mason jars and use country-style containers as holders for candles. Let fresh flowers hang from the trees around you. Serve your boards on wooden crates to keep it rustic and beautiful. Keep the colors in line with the rich, dark hues of the berries and grapes.

Berry Galette with Vanilla Bean Whipped Cream

Pastry

1 ⅓ cups flour

2 tablespoons sugar

Zest of 1 orange

1 teaspoon cinnamon

8 tablespoons chilled butter

3 tablespoons whole milk

Filling

2 cups blackberries

2 cups blueberries

¼ cup sugar

2 tablespoons brown sugar

1 tablespoon orange juice

1 tablespoon cornstarch

1 teaspoon vanilla extract

Pastry

Mix together the flour, sugar, orange zest, and cinnamon in a large mixing bowl.

Using either low pulses in a food processor or your hands, mix or rub the butter into the flour until coarse crumbs form. If using your hands, it is important to keep the butter cold.

Add the milk, and either pulse in a food processor until it comes together or stir with a fork until it begins to form a dough. Gather any loose crumbs together, and divide the dough into 4 shiny balls. Wrap them in plastic wrap and chill in the refrigerator for about an hour.

Preheat oven to 400 degrees F.

Filling

Gently combine the berries, sugars, juice, cornstarch, and vanilla together in a large bowl. Be careful not to break or bruise the berries.

Place a piece of parchment paper on a flat surface and dust with flour. Roll out each dough ball into a 3–4-inch circle. Transfer the parchment and dough onto a baking sheet. Spoon the filling into the middle of the circles, leaving about a 1–2-inch border.

Fold border inward all the way around, creating a small folded edge to catch any juices and keep the filling inside. Bake for 25–30 minutes. Allow to cool for 10–15 minutes before transferring to a serving plate.

Vanilla Bean Whipped Cream

1 pint whipping cream

4 tablespoon sugar

1 vanilla bean

Whip the cream until peaks begin to form. Add sugar.

Slice the vanilla bean down the middle and scrape out the insides into the cream. Whip to evenly distribute sugar and vanilla. Chill. Serve spooned over the warm galettes.

Roasted Mixed Vegetables

SERVES 4

2 beets, peeled and
   quartered

2 carrots, peeled and cut into
   1-inch pieces

1 red onion, peeled and
   quartered

1 head garlic, separated into
   cloves

1 cup cubed butternut
   squash

1 red bell pepper, quartered

2 tablespoons maple syrup

2 tablespoons olive oil

Salt and pepper, to taste

Chili flakes, to taste

Preheat oven to 375 degrees F.

Place all the vegetables into an ovenproof dish. Whisk together the maple syrup, olive oil, salt and pepper, and chili flakes. Pour over the vegetables and stir to coat. Roast for 30–40 minutes, until soft, sweet, and tender. Serve warm.

Bratwurst Sausage with Stone-Ground Mustard

SERVES 4

2 tablespoons olive oil

4 bratwurst sausages

½ cup stone-ground mustard

Preheat oven to 350 degrees F.

In an ovenproof pan, warm the oil over medium heat. Add the sausages and cook for about 15 minutes, until well browned all over. Place pan in oven and finish cooking for another 15–20 minutes.

Serve the sausages hot with the stone-ground mustard.

Homemade Concord Grape Juice

SERVES 4

2 pounds Concord grapes

Water

¼ cup or more honey

Wash and remove the stems from the grapes. Place the grapes in a large pan and crush them with a masher or the back of a fork. Add enough water to the pan so the grapes are just covered. Bring to a high simmer and cook until the skins are soft and the juice is released. Do not boil. This takes about 10 minutes. Stir occasionally.

Strain into a fine-mesh sieve, pressing down on the grapes to release all the juice and water. Strain again using a couple of layers of damp cheesecloth to remove the fine sediment. Pour the juice back into the pan and add honey to taste. Warm gently, making sure not to boil. Once the honey is dissolved, remove from heat and allow to cool. Serve chilled.

culture

the sum total of ways of living built up by a group of human beings and transmitted from one generation to another

BOARD IT UP: Culture boards are reflective of world cuisine and should be the voice of various countries, both in presentation and flavor. Think local markets with spices and colors of the people who cook handed-down recipes from their grandmothers. You want these boards to sing unique, delicious, and tradition.

Citrus Rice

Sweet Potato Pakoras

Mini Samosas with Raita and Tamarind Chutney

Tandoori Roast Chicken Quarters

Pistachio and Mint Kulfi Ice Cream

INDIAN SPICES

INSPIRATION India is an awakening. The myriad sights and sounds make you feel alive and invite conscious arousal. This is food to be eaten with your fingers and experienced with your heart. Be open to the intense flavors, surrender to the sublime complexity of spices, and dive into the vibrancy of India.

STYLING TIPS Use silver to display the richness of the Indian culture with this board. The silver will provide a regal contrast to the colorful foods, and if you can find beautiful henna-inspired cups to accent the board, that would look amazing! Let the spiritual heart of India guide you and you cannot go wrong.

Sweet Potato Pakoras

SERVES 6

1 cup grated sweet potato

1 ¼ cups gram (chick pea) flour

1 cup grated onion

Zest and juice of 1 lemon

¼ teaspoon turmeric

½ teaspoon cumin

½ teaspoon coriander

¼ teaspoon cinnamon

¼ teaspoon chili powder

Salt, to taste

6 to 8 tablespoons water

Oil, for deep-frying

Mango chutney, of choice

Place the sweet potato, flour, onion, lemon zest and juice, spices, and salt into a large mixing bowl and thoroughly combine. Stir in enough water to make a thick, smooth batter.

Heat oil for deep-frying. Drop small spoonfuls of the batter into the hot oil. Deep-fry the pakoras until golden brown and crispy, 3–4 minutes. Remove from oil and drain on paper towels. Serve with garnish of mango chutney.

Pistachio and Mint Kulfi Ice Cream

SERVES 6

1 cup whole milk, divided

½ cup pistachios, blanched

1 cup heavy cream

1 cup sweetened condensed
milk

1 teaspoon cardamom
powder

½ teaspoon cinnamon

½ teaspoon peppermint
extract

2 tablespoons finely
chopped fresh mint
leaves

Additional pistachios

In a food processor, whiz together ½ cup whole milk and pistachios until they form a paste.

In the bowl of a stand mixer, add the heavy cream, condensed milk, remaining whole milk, cardamom, and cinnamon. Mix well.

Add the pistachio paste, peppermint extract, and mint leaves and thoroughly combine.

Churn in an ice cream maker following the manufacturer's instructions. Freeze for about 30 minutes before you serve.

Mini Samosas with Raita and Tamarind Chutney

SERVES 6 TO 8

Dough

1 cup all-purpose flour

½ cup gram (chick pea) flour

1 teaspoon salt

1 tablespoon ghee

6 to 8 tablespoons cold water

Filling

2 tablespoons coconut oil or ghee

½ cup chopped onion

2 cloves garlic, crushed

1 cup frozen peas

1 pound potatoes, cooked and roughly mashed

1 tablespoon garam masala

¼ cup fresh cilantro

1 tablespoon lemon juice

Oil, for frying

Dough

Sift together the flours and salt. Rub the ghee into the flour with your hands until it is well coated. Add the water slowly, working the dough until it pulls together. Knead for 4 minutes on a lightly floured surface. Cover and let rest while you make the filling.

Filling

Heat the oil or ghee in a large pan over medium heat. Add the onion and cook until soft. Add the garlic and cook for another minute. Add the peas, potatoes, garam masala, cilantro, and lemon juice. Mix well. Once cooked, remove from heat.

To Assemble

Divide the dough in half. Section off each half into 8 equal-size balls. Roll out the balls into ¼-inch-thick circles that are about 3 inches in diameter, and then cut in half. Place a heaped scoop of filling in each half and fold into a triangle shape, pressing the edges together. Place samosas on a baking sheet.

Heat the oil to 350 degrees F.

Fry in batches until golden and crisp, 5–10 minutes. Carefully remove from hot oil and drain on paper towels.

Raita

MAKES 1 CUP

½ cup plain yogurt

½ cup peeled, seeded, and grated cucumber

2 tablespoons chopped fresh mint

2 tablespoons chopped fresh cilantro

1 tablespoon minced spring onion

¼ teaspoon coriander

¼ teaspoon cumin

Pinch of nutmeg

Juice of ½ lemon

Salt and pepper, to taste

Tamarind Chutney

MAKES ABOUT 1 CUP

1 cup tamarind paste

1 tablespoon cumin powder

1 tablespoon ginger powder

4 Medjool dates

½ cup packed dark brown sugar

1 teaspoon chili powder

Salt and pepper, to taste

½ cup water

Raita

Mix together all of the ingredients in a small bowl. Chill for 20 minutes before serving.

Tamarind Chutney

Mix together all the ingredients in a saucepan and bring to a simmer. Cook until the dates are soft and breaking apart and the liquid has reduced to about 1 cup. Strain and serve.

Tandoori Roast Chicken Quarters

SERVES 6

2 teaspoons coconut oil

½ teaspoon mustard seeds

½ teaspoon cumin seeds

½ teaspoon nigella seeds

1 tablespoon garlic powder

1 tablespoon ginger powder

1 tablespoon tandoori
    powder

Salt and pepper, to taste

¼ cup plain Greek yogurt

2 pounds chicken quarters

Lemon or lime wedges

Citrus Rice

2 cups basmati rice, well
    rinsed

3 cups vegetable stock

Juice and zest of 1 lemon

Melt the oil in a pan over medium heat. Once hot, add all the seeds and cook until they begin to sizzle and pop. Mix toasted seeds, spices, and salt and pepper into the yogurt. Rub all over the chicken and marinate for at least 2 hours, but overnight is best.

Preheat oven to 350 degrees F.

Place chicken in a roasting pan and roast for about 40 minutes, until juices run clear and the chicken is cooked through. Serve with lemon wedges for garnish.

Citrus Rice

Place rice and stock in a saucepan, cover, and bring to a boil. Once boiling, turn heat down to simmer and cook for 15 minutes. Remove rice from the heat and add the lemon juice and zest; stir well. Let stand for 5–10 minutes then fluff with fork.

Mangos and Sticky Rice

Chicken Satay Sticks

Pickled Veggie Summer Rolls with Ginger Soy Sauce

Thai Broth and Noodles

THAI FLOATING MARKET

INSPIRATION A Thai floating market brings the freshest ingredients from land and sea straight off boats and into your hands. Aromatic spices and sensual coconuts tantalize your senses and should be the basis for the creative color exploration that makes up the foods of this board. In order to create this meal, explore a mixture of exotic flavors in unique combinations that satisfies you on all levels.

STYLING TIPS Make the most of the bold colors and fresh fruits and flowers of a Thai-inspired presentation and bring your board to life. Carrots and cucumbers carved into flowers are simple and beautiful, or use fresh flowers to show off the colors of Thailand.

Chicken Satay Sticks

SERVES 4

Bamboo skewers

4 boneless, skinless chicken breasts

½ cup chopped white onion

2 cloves garlic, crushed

2 tablespoons grated fresh ginger

2 tablespoons soy sauce

1 fresh Thai chile pepper, seeded and diced

1 teaspoon ground coriander

2 teaspoons brown sugar

Juice of 1 lime

1 tablespoon sesame oil

Peanut Dipping Sauce

1 cup coconut milk

¼ cup peanut butter

1 tablespoon fish sauce

1 tablespoon fresh lime juice

Salt and pepper, to taste

Soak bamboo skewers in water for an hour before using. Heat grill.

Trim fat from chicken and pound with a meat mallet to tenderize and thin a little. Cut into long strips and place in a shallow dish.

Mix the onion, garlic, ginger, soy sauce, chile, coriander, brown sugar, lime juice, and oil together in a small bowl. Pour over chicken and chill, marinating for at least 2 hours. This can be done the night before.

Once marinated, thread the chicken onto the bamboo skewers. Grill for about 5 minutes on each side, basting with the marinade.

Peanut Dipping Sauce

Simmer all the ingredients together in a small saucepan over medium heat. If very thick, add a little water. Serve with the chicken satay.

Mangos and Sticky Rice

SERVES 4

½ cup sticky rice (available from Thai markets, can substitute with short-grain rice)

1 cup coconut milk, divided

⅓ cup packed light brown sugar

½ teaspoon salt

4 mangos, peeled, pitted, and sliced

1 teaspoon sesame seeds

Rinse the rice until the water runs clear. Cover the rice with cold water in a bowl and leave to soak overnight.

Line a bamboo steamer with cheesecloth and tip the rice onto it; cover. Steam the rice in the steamer over a pan of boiling water for about 40 minutes.

In a small pan, heat together all but 4 tablespoons of the coconut milk, the brown sugar, and salt.

Place the cooked rice into a bowl and pour the sweet milk over it. Stir and fluff until the rice is coated. Let soak for about 15 minutes.

Scoop out the rice and arrange on a plate with the mango slices. Drizzle remaining coconut milk over the top and sprinkle with the sesame seeds.

Pickled Veggie Summer Rolls with Ginger Soy Sauce

SERVES 4

1 cup julienned carrots

½ cup julienned cucumbers

½ cup julienned radishes 1 jalapeño, thinly sliced

1-inch slice peeled ginger

1 cup rice vinegar

1 cup water

4 tablespoons sugar

½ teaspoon sea salt

3 tablespoons lime juice

1 tablespoon soy sauce

12 spring roll rice papers

1 cup cooked rice noodles

1 package smoked tofu, cut into thin strips

1 large bundle combined cilantro, basil, and mint

¼ cup soy sauce

1 teaspoon hot sauce

1 green onion, thinly sliced

1 teaspoon chopped fresh ginger

Place the julienned vegetables, jalapeño, and ginger in a container or jar that holds them all.

Mix together the vinegar, water, sugar, salt, lime juice, and soy sauce. Pour over the vegetables. Seal the container and shake to meld the ingredients together. Refrigerate for 30 minutes.

Follow the directions on the rice paper package to prepare them for rolling.

Assemble the pickled vegetables, cooked noodles, tofu, herbs, and rice papers in one place for easy use. Reserve ¼ cup of the pickling liquid.

Working on 1 roll at a time, soak the rice paper in water for 15 seconds to become soft and flexible. Remove from water and, working on a slightly damp surface, spread some vegetables, noodles, herbs, and tofu from the left to the right and then roll.

Place each roll with the seam down on your serving board and keep covered with a light, damp towel until ready to serve.

To make a gingery dipping sauce, combine the reserved pickling liquid with the soy sauce, hot sauce, green onion, and chopped ginger.

Thai Broth and Rice Noodles

SERVES 2

1 tablespoon sesame oil

1 shallot, chopped

1 clove garlic, chopped

4 shiitake mushrooms, sliced

4 cups fish or chicken stock

1 tablespoon fish sauce

½ green chile pepper,
    julienned

1 stalk lemongrass, mashed

½-inch piece fresh ginger,
    peeled and thinly sliced

½-inch piece fresh galangal,
    peeled and thinly sliced

1 package rice noodles

1 carrot, thinly sliced

½ red bell pepper, julienned

2 scallions, sliced

1 tablespoon chopped
    cilantro leaves

1 teaspoon sesame seeds

1 fresh lime, cut into wedges

Heat the oil in a large saucepan. Add the shallot and sweat for 1 minute before adding the garlic and mushrooms. Cook for 1 minute more, being careful to not burn the garlic.

Remove from heat then add the stock, fish sauce, half of the chile pepper, lemongrass, ginger, and galangal. Return to heat and bring broth up to a simmer and cook for 10 minutes; set aside.

Cook noodles per package instructions, and then place into a large bowl.

Reheat broth gently then pour over noodles. Garnish with the carrot, bell pepper, scallions, remaining chili pepper, cilantro, and sesame seeds. Serve with lime wedges.

Griddled Lime Zucchini

Carne Asada
Street Tacos

Stuffed Mexican
Chile Peppers

Horchata

Classic Salsa

STREETS OF MEXICO

INSPIRATION Mexican cuisine has many different regions and personalities, and the food and country are a sensual experience of bright colors, earthy spices, and uplifting citrus. This board brings the hustle and vibrant life of a Mexican street fair to the table and to your gathering. Get your mariachi on and let the party begin.

STYLING TIPS Use the streets of Mexico as your map to this board, and throw in parchment paper to house the tacos and maybe even tequila shot glasses for the salsa. Large colored flowers, turquoise colors, and spices can accent this board with the real flavors of this cheerful culture, alluring the diner to truly enjoy these classic flavors.

Carne Asada Street Tacos

SERVES 6

3 cups orange juice

1 head garlic, peeled and smashed

¼ cup lime juice

¼ cup pickled jalapeños

1 bunch cilantro, chopped and divided

1 ½ cups chopped onions, divided

1 tablespoon cumin

1 teaspoon salt

1 teaspoon cracked pepper

2 pounds skirt or flank steak

6 (4- to 6-inch) corn tortillas

Mix together the orange juice, garlic, lime juice, jalapeños, half of the cilantro, 1 cup of the onions, cumin, salt, and pepper to make a marinade.

Place the steak into a gallon-size ziplock bag. Pour the marinade over the meat and refrigerate for at least 2 hours, and up to 24–48 hours.

When ready to cook, heat your grill to medium high and oil it. Cook the meat for about 7 minutes on each side. Remove the steak to a cutting board and let rest for 5–10 minutes. Once rested, slice the steak across the grain into strips. You can serve like this or chop into smaller pieces.

Warm the tortillas and layer the meat on them.

Mix the remaining onion and cilantro together and top each taco with the garnish.

Classic Salsa

SERVES 6

1 cup diced tomatoes

1 cup diced tomatillos

1 cup diced onion

1 jalapeño, seeded and
   diced

1 clove garlic, crushed

Juice of 1 lime

1 bunch fresh cilantro,
   chopped

Salt, to taste

Pepper, to taste

Tortilla chips

Combine the tomatoes, tomatillos, onion, jalapeño, garlic, lime juice, and cilantro in a blender and purée. Check for seasonings and add salt and pepper as needed.

Serve with tortilla chips.

Stuffed Mexican Chile Peppers

SERVES 6

6 Anaheim peppers

½ cup peeled, deveined,
    and roughly chopped
    jumbo shrimp

½ cup crumbled Cotija
    cheese

½ cup grated Monterey
    Jack cheese, plus extra

½ cup salsa verde

Preheat oven to 375 degrees F, and slit open the peppers lengthwise so you can seed and stuff them. The peppers needs to have a little pocket, so make sure not to cut all the way through.

Mix together the shrimp, cheeses, and salsa in a bowl. Stuff each pepper with the mix and top with a little extra Monterey Jack cheese. Place in a baking dish and cook for 20–30 minutes, until the cheese is melted and lightly browned.

Griddled Lime Zucchini

SERVES 6

2 pounds zucchini, sliced into
    thin rounds

3 tablespoons olive oil

Salt and pepper, to taste

8 lime wedges

Coat the zucchini in the oil, and season with salt and pepper.

Cook zucchini on a hot, oiled griddle pan until hot and seared with griddle marks. Squeeze with lime wedges and transfer to a serving board.

Horchata

SERVES 6

1 ½ cups uncooked long-
    grain white rice

1 Mexican cinnamon stick

1 cup blanched almonds

1 teaspoon nutmeg

4 cups water

½ cup sugar

Place the rice, cinnamon, almonds, and nutmeg in a food processor and blend to a crumbly powder texture.

Place the powder in a clean airtight jar and top with the water. Stir well and cover. Let sit at room temperature for about 12 hours, or overnight.

.Pour the mixture into a blender and add sugar. Blend until smooth, and then strain the solids out using a fine-mesh sieve or cheesecloth. Discard the solids.

Serve the Horchata chilled.

INDEX

ACKNOWLEDGMENTS

I want to give a very special shout-out to Jessica Booth, who helped in the creation of these recipes and who is an amazing friend, confidant, and soul sister! You are the best. Thank you, Alexandra, for being in the creative zone with me in order to get this book to the level of beauty it deserves!

To Michelle at Gibbs Smith, thank you for believing in me for this project and for your support and guidance. I adore you.

ANNI DAULTER is a professional cook, food and beauty way stylist, and author. She founded the baby food company Bohemian Baby and is the founder of the Sacred Living Movement. She has styled food for several books, including *Meringue*, *Caramel*, *The French Cook*, and *Mashed*, as well as authored *The Organic Family Cookbook*, *Ice Pop Joy*, *Sacred Relationship*, *Sacred Pregnancy Deck*, and others. She lives in Boulder, Colorado, with her family.

METRIC CONVERSION CHART

VOLUME MEASUREMENTS		WEIGHT MEASUREMENTS		TEMPERATURE CONVERSION	
U.S.	Metric	U.S.	Metric	Fahrenheit	Celsius
1 teaspoon	5 ml	½ ounce	15 g	250	120
1 tablespoon	15 ml	1 ounce	30 g	300	150
¼ cup	60 ml	3 ounces	90 g	325	160
⅓ cup	75 ml	4 ounces	115 g	350	180
½ cup	125 ml	8 ounces	225 g	375	190
⅔ cup	150 ml	12 ounces	350 g	400	200
¾ cup	175 ml	1 pound	450 g	425	220
1 cup	250 ml	2¼ pounds	1 kg	450	230